NORTHERN ITALY TRAVEL GUIDE 2025

Discover Stunning Lakes Mountains and Cities in One Trip

LILLY DAVEY

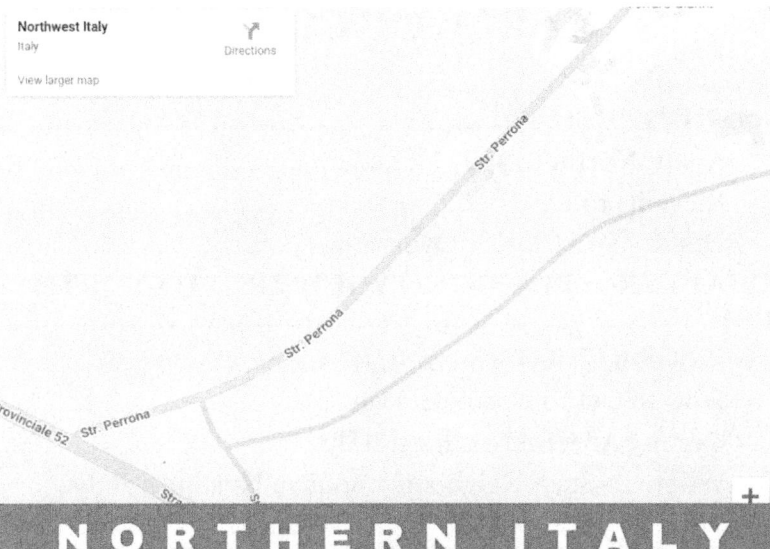

Northwest Italy
Italy
View larger map
Directions

Str. Perrona
Str. Perrona
Provinciale 52   Str. Perrona

N O R T H E R N   I T A L Y

SCAN QR CODE

- Open your phone's camera app
- Point camera at the QR code
- Hold steady until your phone recognizes it
- Tap the pop-up notification when it appears
- View the content that opens automatically

TABLE OF CONTENTS

INTRODUCTION

Welcome to your journey through Northern Italy, where every cobblestone tells a story and every sunset paints the ancient towers in hues of gold and rose. I'm thrilled to share this corner of the world with you – a place where art, history, and daily life dance together in perfect harmony. Let me take you through my own love affair with this enchanting region.

My first morning in Milan still feels like yesterday. The early light was streaming through the intricate spires of the Duomo as I sipped my first proper Italian cappuccino at the historic Camparino in Galleria. The barista's practiced hands crafted a perfect foam heart, and elderly gentlemen in impeccable suits read their morning papers at the marble counter. That's when I realized – this wasn't going to be just another trip. This was going to be an immersion into a way of life.

Venice came next, and oh, what a revelation! Getting lost is an art form here. One afternoon, I wandered away from the crowds near St. Mark's and found myself in Cannaregio, where laundry lines stretched across narrow canals and children played soccer in tiny squares. An old woman was feeding cats on her doorstep, and the scent of fresh bread led me to a tiny bakery where the owner insisted I try his still warm focaccia. These aren't the moments you plan for – they're the ones that find you.

The lakes captivated me in a unique way. At Lake Como, I stayed in a centuries-old villa turned hotel, where the breakfast room's windows framed the water like Renaissance paintings. One morning, I took a wooden boat ride with Marco, a third generation boat maker who spoke about the lake's moods as if describing an old friend. The mist rolled across the water, revealing and concealing the shoreline's pastel villages, each one more charming than the last.

Turin surprised me with its elegance. Under its famous porticoes, I discovered a city of dreamers and inventors. In a historic café, where mirrors and marble transported me to another era, I learned about the tradition of bicerin – a layered drink of coffee, chocolate, and cream that's been serving comfort in a glass since the 18th century. The elderly proprietor told me stories of writers and politicians who had sat at these very tables, planning Italy's future over cups of coffee.

The countryside of Piedmont painted autumn in new colors for me. In Alba, I joined a truffle hunter and his dog at dawn. The morning fog (they call it nebbia here) wrapped around the hillsides like a silk scarf, and the excitement of finding a white truffle hidden in the earth was absolutely infectious. That evening, in a tiny restaurant where the menu was simply what the grandmother felt like cooking that day, I tasted pasta that brought tears to my eyes – the truffle we'd found shaved over it like snowflakes.

In Verona, I learned that romance goes beyond Romeo and Juliet. It's in the way the afternoon light hits the pink marble of the Roman arena, in the laughter echoing from courtyard restaurants, and in the passion with which locals debate the best place for gelato. I found mine – a tiny shop where the pistachio was made from nuts brought in from Sicily, and the dark chocolate was so intense it was almost black.

The memories blend like watercolors – the first time I tasted properly aged ParmigianoReggiano in Modena, watching the master craftsman crack open a wheel like it was a book of secrets. The afternoon I spent with an elderly couple in their Bologna apartment, learning to roll pasta so thin you could see the wood of the table through it. The sunset that turned the marble quarries of Carrara into mirrors of gold.

This is Northern Italy – not just a destination, but a feeling. It's in the way strangers become friends over a shared plate of risotto alla Milanese, in the sound of church bells echoing across ancient squares, and in the stories told by stones that have witnessed centuries of history. Every time I return, I discover something new, yet it always feels like coming home.

Come join me. Let these places weave their magic into your own story. Slow down. Look up at the frescoed ceilings. Accept that invitation to a family dinner. Say yes to the mystery pasta special. Northern Italy isn't a checklist of sights to see – it's a collection of moments waiting to become memories, a place where beauty isn't just in the monuments but in the minutes between them.

And as you plan your own journey, remember – the best stories often begin when you put down the map and follow your curiosity. Every corner of Northern Italy holds a thousand stories. I've shared mine; now it's time for you to create yours.

About Northern Italy

In the embrace of the mighty Alps and the gentle lap of the Adriatic Sea lies a land where innovation and tradition dance an eternal waltz. Northern Italy isn't just a geographical designation – it's where Roman emperors once moved their capital from Rome to Milan, recognizing the strategic brilliance of this position at Europe's crossroads.

The story of this region is written in the rocks of the Dolomites, where ancient coral reefs thrust skyward became pink hued mountains, and in the depths of subalpine lakes carved by glaciers. These waters, especially Lake Garda, create their own microclimate, allowing olive trees and citrus groves to flourish at latitudes that normally wouldn't support Mediterranean vegetation. Here, you'll find lemon houses – limonaie – historic greenhouse structures unique to Lake Garda's western shore, where citrus has been cultivated since the 13th century.

This is a land of surprising contrasts. In the Po Valley, rice paddies stretch to the horizon – the largest rice producing region in Europe, where generations of mondine (women rice workers) once sang ancient songs while planting the grains that would become creamy risotto. The same valley hosts some of Europe's most advanced agricultural technology, where centuries old farming techniques meet precision agriculture.

The region's waterways tell tales of ingenuity. Leonardo da Vinci himself designed Milan's navigli, a network of canals that transformed the city into a maritime power despite being landlocked. Today, some of these engineering marvels still operate, including the incredible Naviglio Pavese, which uses a series of locks to navigate a 56 meter drop in elevation between Milan and Pavia.

Northern Italy's contribution to world culture extends far beyond the expected. The University of Bologna, founded in 1088, pioneered the concept of academic freedom and created the modern university system. In Cremona, the Stradivari family didn't just make violins – they unlocked the secrets of wood and sound that still mystify scientists today. The local spruce trees they used, from Val di Fiemme's "Forest of Violins," still supply wood to the world's finest instrument makers.

In the textile heartlands around Como and Biella, silk weaving traditions dating back to the 15th century evolved into today's haute couture. The clear mountain water here proved perfect for silk processing, leading to innovations in textile manufacturing that still influence global fashion. Biella's woodworking heritage stretches back two millennia, with water so pure it became known as the "golden fleece capital."

The region's marble quarries at Carrara, where Michelangelo chose the block for his David, reveal their own fascinating world. The "marble roads" – rails carved directly into the mountain – showcase how ancient Romans ingeniously transported massive blocks using olive oil and wooden rollers. Modern quarries now use diamond tipped wires to cut marble with surgical precision, while maintaining age old techniques for identifying the finest blocks.

Underground, Northern Italy holds more secrets.The Po Valley, situated in Northern Italy, is home to Europe's most substantial natural gas reserves, a discovery dating back to the 1940s. This discovery helped fuel Italy's postwar economic miracle. Meanwhile, in Alba, the unique combination of soil composition and microclimate creates the perfect environment for the rare white truffle, making this small town the world's truffle capital.

The influence of Northern Italy's innovative spirit reaches far beyond its borders. The region gave birth to the first public bank (Monte dei Paschi di Siena, 1472), pioneered the double entry bookkeeping system through Luca Pacioli, and revolutionized modern architecture through Palladio's designs. The world's first industrial scale electricity distribution began here, when the Acquedotto De FerrariGalliera began powering Genoa's port in 1892.

Even the fog that frequently blankets the Po Valley plays its part in the region's unique character. This nebbia contributes to the aging process of cured meats and cheeses, adding subtle flavors that can't be replicated elsewhere. Local winemakers in regions like Barolo embrace the fog as an essential element in developing their wines' complex personalities.

The linguistic landscape is equally fascinating. The region's GalloItalic languages preserve ancient Celtic influences, while the Ladin language, spoken in the Dolomites, maintains traces of the Roman Empire's Vulgar Latin. In the Cimbrian language islands of the Venetian Alps, medieval German dialects survive, testament to the region's role as a crossroads of European cultures.

Modern Northern Italy continues to innovate while honoring its past. The region leads Italy in renewable energy production, with the TrentinoAlto Adige region generating 90% of its electricity from renewable sources. Historic water mills are being repurposed as small hydroelectric plants, while ancient Roman forums house cutting edge technology startups.

This is Northern Italy – where every innovation has a story stretching back centuries, and every tradition points toward the future. It's a land where scientists study the acoustics of Renaissance churches to understand perfect sound, and where space age materials are tested in workshops that once crafted armor for medieval knights. Here, the past doesn't just survive – it evolves, innovates, and continues to shape the future.

Reasons to Love

The magic of Northern Italy seeps into your soul through countless small moments that unfold in daily life. Each morning begins with the ritual of perfectly crafted espresso and warm brioche from century old bakeries, where the scent of fresh baked pastries mingles with the sound of animated conversations. The ancient porticoed walkways of Bologna stretch for forty kilometers, sheltering residents as they've done for centuries, while evening passeggiata transform quiet streets into vibrant social scenes where entire communities emerge to stroll, chat, and share in the tradition of aperitivo.

Nature puts on a spectacular show here, painting the Dolomites in shades of rose during alpenglow, a phenomenon that transforms harsh rocky peaks into ethereal sculptures at dawn and dusk. Along Lake Como, patient observers might catch the mysterious "green ray" at sunset, while summer evenings in the rice fields near Vercelli come alive with dancing fireflies. Hidden thermal springs in Bormio still bubble up where Romans once bathed beneath star filled skies, offering a timeless connection to the region's ancient past.

The land holds endless secrets waiting to be discovered. Turin's underground rivers influenced its esoteric architecture, creating a mysterious underworld beneath its elegant streets. Medieval herb gardens, still tended by monks using techniques passed down through millennia, preserve ancient botanical knowledge. In Venice, hidden passageways in old palazzos lead to traditional squeri where craftsmen build gondolas using methods unchanged for centuries, while village church sundials still keep perfect time using nothing but shadow and stone.

Cultural traditions here don't just survive – they thrive. Village festivals celebrate everything from cheese to chestnuts with rituals that date back generations. Historic wine windows (buchette del vino) in palace walls, once used to serve wine during plagues, tell stories of resilience and adaptation. Bell towers ring melodies that have echoed through these valleys since the Renaissance, while local dialects preserve words that capture emotions no other language can express.

The culinary landscape reads like a love letter to tradition and territory. Each village around the Po Valley proudly maintains its own unique rice varieties, while mountain cheeses age in caves with naturally perfect humidity. Traditional balsamic vinegar, aged longer than many fine wines, becomes a family's liquid legacy, passed down through generations along with carefully guarded recipe books filled with handwritten notes and cooking secrets.

Architectural innovation spans millennia here. Roman bridges still carry daily traffic, while Renaissance buildings demonstrate sophisticated natural air conditioning systems that put modern technology to shame. In Como, historic water wheels continue to power silk mills, maintaining a connection to the region's textile heritage. Alpine churches preserve priceless frescoes thanks to perfect microclimates created by clever medieval architects.

Craftsmanship reaches levels of near mystical devotion. In Cremona, violin makers select wood from the same forest that supplied Stradivari, while Murano's glass blowers practice techniques passed down through 700 years of family history. Paper makers in Fabriano still create watermarks using medieval methods, and in Carrara's marble quarries, sculptors follow the same veins of stone first mapped by Michelangelo.

The blend of old and new creates something entirely unique. Historic palazzos house cutting edge design studios, while ancient monasteries have been transformed into world class research facilities. Traditional farming techniques merge with sustainable agriculture, creating a future that honors the past. Renaissance water systems find new life powering eco-friendly initiatives.

Each season brings its own enchantment. Spring carpets Vignola's hills in cherry blossoms, creating ephemeral pink snowfalls. Summer evenings fill Roman amphitheaters with music, while autumn brings the ancient ritual of truffle hunting with dogs from generations old bloodlines. Winter transforms thermal baths into magical retreats with views of snow capped peaks.

The social fabric here remains strong and vibrant. Multigenerational families still gather for Sunday lunches that stretch into evening, while village festivals unite entire communities in celebrations where everyone from children to grandparents plays a vital role. Your local coffee bar becomes a second home, where your regular order is remembered by heart and friendly faces greet you each morning.

In Northern Italy, even the simplest moments carry profound beauty. Whether you're discovering a masterpiece hidden in a village church, sharing a candlelit dinner in a converted medieval cloister, or simply watching sunset paint the lakes in gold, each experience adds another reason to fall in love with this extraordinary corner of the world.

History and Culture Overview

Long before Italy existed as a unified nation, Northern Italy was shaping European history through its powerful city states and merchant republics. This land, once known as Cisalpine Gaul, witnessed Celtic settlements blend with Roman ambition, creating unique cultural crossroads that would influence centuries of art, commerce, and innovation. When Rome's emperors moved their capital to Milan in 286 CE, they recognized what many had known before – this region held the keys to controlling both the Alpine passes and the fertile Po Valley.

The arrival of the Lombards in the 6th century left an indelible mark on the region's character. These Germanic warriors became sophisticated rulers, establishing Pavia as their capital and creating a complex system of laws that would influence European legal traditions for centuries. Their legacy lives on not just in the name Lombardy, but in the region's distinct architectural style, which married northern European sensibilities with Mediterranean aesthetics.

The Middle Ages saw the rise of independent communes, where an emergent merchant class challenged feudal power and established new forms of civic governance. Venice built its maritime empire, controlling trade routes to the East, while Genoa's bankers financed European monarchs. The University of Bologna, founded in 1088, pioneered the concept of academic freedom and attracted scholars from across Europe, establishing a tradition of intellectual excellence that would help spark the Renaissance.

This cultural rebirth found fertile ground in Northern Italy's courts and cities. The powerful families of Milan (the Visconti and Sforza), Ferrara (the Este), and Mantua (the Gonzaga) all played a significant role in the

Renaissance as patrons of the arts and humanist scholars.Leonardo da Vinci found sanctuary in Milan, where he painted The Last Supper and filled notebooks with innovations centuries ahead of their time. In Mantua, Andrea Mantegna created illusionistic masterpieces that would influence artists for generations.

The region's musical heritage runs equally deep. In Cremona, the Amati family established a school of violin making that would reach its apex with Antonio Stradivari, whose instruments remain unmatched. Venice's musical traditions gave birth to the modern opera house, while its carnival celebrations inspired composers across Europe. Each city developed its own musical identity, from the sacred compositions of the Venetian School to the innovative operas of Milan's La Scala.

Religious architecture tells its own fascinating story. The great cathedrals of Milan and Modena showcase different interpretations of faith and power – Milan's Gothic spires reaching heavenward while Modena's Romanesque dignity speaks of earthly authority. Countless smaller churches house artistic treasures and tell tales of local saints, while abbeys in the countryside preserve ancient manuscripts and agricultural knowledge.

The industrial revolution transformed Northern Italy once again. Turin became Italy's first capital and its automotive heart, while Milan established itself as a global fashion capital. The region's entrepreneurial spirit, built on centuries of merchant tradition, created an industrial triangle between Turin, Milan, and Genoa that would drive Italy's economic miracle after World War II.

Yet beneath this modernization, ancient traditions endure. The region's linguistic heritage preserves traces of Celtic, Germanic, and Latin influences, with each valley often maintaining its distinct dialect. Food traditions tell stories of conquest, trade, and adaptation – risotto speaking to Arab influence in rice cultivation, while Germanic spices appear in northern Italian Christmas treats.

Craftsmanship remains a defining cultural characteristic. In Venice's Murano, glassmakers still guard centuries old secrets. Como's silk weavers maintain traditions that made the region a textile powerhouse. In countless small workshops, artisans practice skills passed down through generations, from woodcarving to metalwork, each piece telling a story of dedication to beauty and function.

The rhythm of life here still follows ancient patterns. Market days in small towns bring farmers and artisans together as they have for centuries. Religious festivals mark the calendar with processions and celebrations that unite entire communities. Even modern business practices often reflect medieval traditions – many of the region's most successful companies remain family owned, passing specialized knowledge from generation to generation.

Water shapes both landscape and culture. The great lakes have long provided natural climate control, allowing Mediterranean plants to flourish at the foot of the Alps. Venice's relationship with the sea created unique traditions and technologies, while the Po River's vast plain became one of Europe's most productive agricultural regions. Ancient irrigation systems, some dating to Roman times, still water fields and gardens.

Today, Northern Italy's culture continues to evolve while maintaining deep connections to its past. Historic palazzos house innovative startups, while traditional craftspeople embrace new technologies. Universities founded in the Middle Ages lead research into artificial intelligence and sustainable energy. This ability to bridge past and future, tradition and innovation, remains perhaps the region's most remarkable cultural achievement – creating a living laboratory where history doesn't just survive but actively shapes the future.

CHAPTER 1: PLANNING YOUR TRIP TO NORTHERN ITALY

Northern Italy welcomes visitors year round, though spring and fall steal the show with mild weather and fewer crowds. Major airports in Milan, Venice, and Bologna offer easy access, while the region's excellent train network makes hopping between cities a breeze. Pack layers regardless of season – you might need both sunglasses and a light jacket on the same day. Most travelers find comfort in historic centers or charming residential areas, where boutique hotels and family run B&Bs provide authentic stays without breaking the bank.

Traveling here is straightforward for most visitors – EU citizens can enter freely, while others typically need a Schengen visa, easily arranged through Italian embassies worldwide. The euro is your companion throughout the region, and while Italian prevails, English is widely spoken in tourist areas and international businesses. Pre Booking through trusted platforms like local hotel websites or recognized travel providers helps secure better rates, especially during peak seasons like summer and major events.

Smart travelers can stretch their euros by mixing simple trattorias with occasional splurges, exploring lesser known towns alongside famous destinations, and taking advantage of city passes that include transport and museums. A daily budget of €100150 covers comfortable accommodation, good meals, and sightseeing, though you can spend less by choosing family run guesthouses and local markets, or more if luxury hotels and Michelin Starred restaurants call your name. Keep an eye out for early bird museum tickets, regional train passes, and offseason hotel rates to make the most of your northern Italian adventure.

When to Visit Northern Italy

Northern Italy dances to the rhythm of four distinct seasons, each painting the landscape in its own palette and bringing unique celebrations to life. The timing of your visit shapes not just what you'll see, but what you'll taste, experience, and remember forever.

Early spring arrives with the ancient flower markets of Milan's Navigli district, where canalside vendors have sold bulbs and blooms since the 18th century. March brings the first whispers of warmth to Lake Garda, where unique microclimates allow citrus groves to flourish beneath medieval stone walls. By April, the Langhe hills burst into a symphony of wild orchids, and lucky visitors might spot the rare Alpine snowbells pushing through melting snow in the Dolomites.

May unfolds with the spectacle of the rose moon over Venice, when full moonlight transforms the lagoon into liquid silver. This is when local fishermen still practice the ancient art of mercante – traditional soft shell crab harvesting that follows the lunar calendar. The mild temperatures make it perfect for discovering hidden cloisters and monastery gardens, where herbs used in traditional liqueurs begin their growing season.

Summer arrives with the sweet scent of jasmine in Turin's elegant squares. June sees the start of the quintessentially Italian rite of aperitivo all'aperto – outdoor evening drinks that transform historic piazzas into openair salons. In July, the Alpine meadows above Bolzano explode with rare edelweiss and fire lilies, while mountain huts open their doors for the ancient tradition of alpeggio, when cows are moved to high pastures and cheesemaking becomes a daily ritual.

August brings the mysterious phenomenon of green nights in the Po Delta, where bioluminescent plankton create ethereal displays in the water. While Italian cities empty for Ferragosto (August 15th), mountain villages come alive with sagre – food festivals celebrating single ingredients like the prized cardoons of Piedmont or the violet asparagus of Albenga.

The vineyards are ablaze with incredible shades of gold and crimson in autumn.September is marked by the harvest moon, when centuries old estates still time their grape picking to lunar phases. October brings the white truffle season to Alba, accompanied by medieval fairs were flamethrowers perform ancient choreographies. In November, the morning fog transforms the rice fields around Vercelli into mystical landscapes, while local families gather for the traditional pig slaughter that will produce next year's prosciutto.

Winter arrives with the first snowfall over Milan's Duomo, its golden Madonnina glinting against leaden skies. December illuminates ancient porticoed streets with traditional lighting festivals, while thermal towns like Bormio invite visitors to soak in steaming outdoor pools surrounded by snowy peaks. January sees the curious tradition of the Marry Month in Venice's Cannaregio district, when local bachelors once proposed by floating oranges to their beloved's windows.

The seasons here aren't just about weather – they orchestrate everything from fishing practices to cheese production. Summer evenings mean impromptu classical concerts in Roman ruins, while winter months bring the centuries old tradition of veggia – when neighbors gather in the warmest house to share stories and preserve summer fruits.

Each month carries its own gifts: the first spring peas served with ancient rice varieties, summer evenings scented with night blooming jasmine, autumn's porcini emerging after mountain rains, and winter's chestnut harvest smoked in traditional graa – cone shaped stone structures that dot mountain villages.

The regional microclimates create fascinating seasonal variations. While Venice might be wrapped in mysterious winter mists, the nearby Euganean Hills enjoy a Mediterranean climate where olive trees flourish. Lake Como's infamous winds – the Tivano in the morning and Breva in the afternoon – regulate sailing traditions that haven't changed since Roman times.

For those seeking unique experiences, consider the shoulder seasons' special offerings. Late spring brings the transumanza, when shepherds move their flocks to mountain pastures along ancient routes, while early autumn offers the chance to participate in grape harvests at historic wineries where traditional footpressing is still practiced.

Weather patterns here tell stories of cultural adaptation. The thick fog that blankets the Po Valley in winter created a tradition of slow cooked dishes perfect for cold days, while the fierce summer sun gave birth to the custom of riposo – the afternoon pause that sees towns fall quiet in the heat of the day, only to come alive again at dusk.

How to Get to Northern Italy

The journey to Northern Italy becomes part of the adventure itself, with each arrival point offering its own unique introduction to this captivating region. Milan's Malpensa Airport, built on ancient Roman roads, welcomes visitors with its Volandia Museum nearby, housing rare aircraft in historic hangars where Italy's first aviation pioneers tested their flying machines. The lesser known Bergamo Airport, originally a World War II military base, now serves as a gateway to the Alps, with arrival routes offering breathtaking views of snow capped peaks on clear days.

Venice Marco Polo Airport presents perhaps the world's most theatrical arrival – touch down where Republic galleons once sailed, then choose between arriving by water taxi across the lagoon (following ancient trading routes) or the futuristic People Mover that glides above reclaimed renaissance gardens. For those seeking secret shortcuts, the tiny Treviso Airport connects to Venice via historic Roman roads, now transformed into cycling paths that parallel your bus route.

Train journeys into Northern Italy unveil epic engineering feats. The TurinLyon high speed line burrows through the Alps via the historic Fréjus Rail Tunnel, first carved in 1871, while the Brenner Pass route from Austria descends through 64 bridges and 20 tunnels, each a testament to human ingenuity. The legendary Orient Express still occasionally graces these tracks, though today's high speed Frecciarossa trains slash journey times while offering wine tastings of vintages from passing regions.

For those driving, the Great St. Bernard Pass – Europe's oldest alpine pass, used by Napoleon's armies – offers a dramatic entry into Valle d'Aosta. The more serene Simplon Pass reveals the first glimpse of Mediterranean vegetation meeting Alpine landscapes. Modern AutoStrade follow ancient Roman roads, with service areas often built near archaeological sites – the A1 autogrill near Fiorenzuola sits atop a Roman way station, while the one near Piacenza offers views of medieval pilgrim routes.

Cruise ships dock in Genoa's historic port, where Christopher Columbus learned navigation, or Venice's Marittima terminal, built on artificial islands created by the Republic's engineers in the 15th century. Lesserknown ports like Trieste welcome ships where Habsburg emperors once arrived, its unique blend of Italian, Slavic, and Austrian culture evident from the first glimpse of its shore.

Adventure seekers might choose mountain passes on motorcycles or bicycles. The Stelvio Pass, with its 48 hairpin turns, challenges riders where 19thcentury stagecoaches once carried European aristocrats to alpine spa towns. The gentler Splüga Pass follows an ancient Roman mule track, now a scenic route connecting Switzerland to Lake Como.

Hikers can still enter Northern Italy on foot through historic pilgrim paths. The Via Francigena, marked by ancient hostels and monasteries, leads through mountain passes where medieval travelers sought shelter. Modern walkers find these same refuges transformed into welcoming guesthouses, some still run by religious orders maintaining centuriesold hospitality traditions.

For private pilots, the Aosta Valley airport sits beneath Mont Blanc, while Como's seaplane base – one of Europe's oldest continuously operating water aerodromes – offers splashdowns where pioneering aviators once tested flying boats. The tiny altiport of Chamois, Europe's highest landing strip, serves a carfree village accessible only by aircraft or cable car.

Even practical transfer options hold hidden charm. The Malpensa Express train winds through the Ticino Natural Park, where herons nest in medieval rice paddies. Airport buses to Bergamo's upper town follow the path of ancient funiculars, while water buses from Venice's airport pass islets where quarantined ships once waited to enter the lagoon.

Contemporary innovations complement historic routes. Electric charging stations now dot ancient Roman rest stops, while highspeed rail hubs incorporate solar panels designed to echo the geometry of Renaissance gardens. Modern bus terminals often connect to historic city gates, where today's travelers enter through the same arches that welcomed medieval merchants.

The variety of entry points creates different first impressions: Milan's airports introduce Italy's economic powerhouse, Venice's waterborne arrival channels centuries of maritime glory, while Alpine crossings reveal the magnificent natural barriers that shaped Northern Italian culture. Each route carries its own stories, from ancient salt roads to modern railway tunnels, offering travelers their first taste of the region's rich historical layers.

Getting Around Northern Italy

Northern Italy's transportation network tells a story of innovation spanning millennia, where Roman roads meet bullet trains and renaissance waterways serve modern vaporetti. The region's unique geography – from Alpine peaks to Mediterranean shores – has inspired ingenious solutions for moving people and goods across dramatically different terrains.

The high speed rail network operates on tracks that often parallel ancient Via Consularis. The stretch between Bologna and Milan runs alongside the Via Emilia, where mile markers from 187 BCE can still be spotted from train windows. Modern stations like Turin's Porta Susa feature glass galleries built directly above archaeological remains of the Roman road system, visible through transparent floor panels.

Local trains reveal hidden treasures that fast services speed past. The Centovalli Railway connecting Domodossola to Locarno winds through chestnut forests on stone viaducts built by Italian migrants returning from America in the 1920s. The Bernina Express climbs from palm trees to glaciers, while the historic VigezzinaCentovalli line connects 83 bridges and 31 tunnels, each an engineering marvel from the Belle Époque.

In Venice, traditional traghetti (gondola ferries) still cross the Grand Canal at points established in the 13th century, charging just €2 for a standing crossing. Modern vaporetti follow routes mapped out by the Republic's trade galleys, while water taxis zip through smaller canals once used by vegetable boats from Sant'Erasmo, the lagoon's ancient garden island.

Milan's historic tram network operates some of the world's oldest continually running streetcars – the beloved "ventotto" trams from the 1920s still clatter along original Art Nouveau routes. The city's underground tells its own tales, with stations doubling as archaeological museums displaying ruins discovered during construction. Line 5's Tre Torri station showcases medieval waterways that once connected to Leonardo da Vinci's navigli system.

Mountain transport combines tradition with innovation. The world's steepest funicular railway in Como, built in 1894, still uses its original counterweight water ballast system. In the Dolomites, old military supply routes from World War I have been transformed into scenic cable car journeys, while mule tracks used by smugglers now serve as hiking paths between Italy and Switzerland.

For cyclists, the ancient towpaths along the navigli (canals) offer traffic free routes between cities. The Ciclopista del Sole follows Roman roads from Brenner Pass to Bologna, incorporating sections of medieval pilgrim routes. Venice's outlying islands can be explored by bike routes that trace the lagoon's ancient salt gathering paths.

Bus networks reach remote villages using roads that haven't changed course since Roman times. The journey from Turin to Sestriere follows switchbacks engineered for horse drawn carriages, while services to Alto Adige's wine country trace paths established by Germanic wine merchants in the Middle Ages.

Lake transportation preserves centuries old traditions. Lake Como's Navigazione operates boats that dock at Liberty Style jetties unchanged since the Grand Tour era. Lake Garda's hydrofoils zoom past locations where ancient Romans built vacation villas, while Lake Maggiore's elegant white fleet has carried passengers to the Borromean Islands since the Belle Époque.

Urban mobility innovations blend past and present. Bologna's extensive porticoes – originally built to expand medieval living space above public walkways – now shelter modern pedestrian routes from sun and rain. Turin's grid system, laid out by Romans and refined by baroque planners, makes navigation intuitive for today's travelers.

For drivers, the autostrade network follows ancient trade routes, with service stations often built near historic rest stops. The A7 motorway from Milan to Genoa traces the Salt Road used since Etruscan times, while the A22 Brenner Motorway parallels a route used by medieval German emperors heading to Rome for coronation.

Modern additions complement historical infrastructure. Bike Sharing stations pop up beneath Renaissance loggias, electric car charging points occupy spaces where horses once watered, and digital journey planners incorporate centuries old shortcuts through monastery gardens and palace courtyards.

Even air travel within the region holds historical significance. Seaplane services on Lake Como use bases established in 1913, when Italy's first seaplane pilots trained here. Mountain helipads occupy sites where mule trains once rested, providing vital links to Alpine communities during winter months.

The future of transport here respects the past while embracing innovation. New light rail lines incorporate archaeological displays, bike paths follow ancient roman roads, and electric buses glide past medieval towers. This layering of old and new creates a transportation network that's both cuttingedge and deeply rooted in history, making every journey a chance to travel through time as well as space.

Where to Stay: Neighbourhoods in Northern Italy

Northern Italy's neighborhoods each tell their own story, from medieval merchants' quarters to hidden artistic havens. Rather than just choosing a place to sleep, selecting the right neighborhood means becoming part of a living community with its own rhythms, traditions, and secrets.

In Milan, the Navigli district pulses with life along its historic canals, where traditional botteghe (artisan workshops) operate below apartments with interior courtyards that once housed silk weavers. Morning light reveals elderly residents tending centuries old grape vines that climb palace walls, while enterprising artists have transformed old boat repair shops into galleries. The lesser known Isola quarter, once a working class island separated by railroad tracks, now hosts weekly street art performances in spaces where partisan resistance fighters once hid.

Venice's Cannaregio reveals a different face of the floating city. Here, kosher bakeries perfume narrow calli with the scent of traditional Jewish sweets, while traditional forcole (gondola oarlock) craftsmen work in studios unchanged for centuries. In the evenings, local bars serve sarde in saor following recipes passed down since the Republic's glory days. The quieter Castello district harbors the city's traditional green spaces – gardens hidden behind monastery walls where elderly residents still grow herbs for traditional remedies.

Turin's Roman Quarter overlays modern life on ancient foundations, with coffee shops occupying spaces where Roman senators once debated. The trendy San Salvario district, built by Savoy architects, mixes Art Nouveau mansions with multicultural markets, while hidden courtyards host jazz concerts where carriage houses once stood. In the Quadrilatero Romano, morning shoppers browse stalls set up beneath baroque porticoes, just as their ancestors did centuries ago.

Bologna's historic Jewish Ghetto weaves through medieval towers, its narrow streets designed to provide shade in summer and shelter in winter. The University district buzzes with Europe's oldest academic traditions – some cafes here have served scholars since the Renaissance. The Cirenaica quarter, named by workers returning from Libya in the 1920s, preserves working class traditions in its community gardens and social clubs.

Verona's ancient artisan quarter, San Zeno, centers around its magnificent Romanesque basilica, where local metalworkers still craft decorative pieces in workshops passed down through generations. The lesser visited Veronetta district, across the Roman bridge, houses frescoed palazzi converted into student apartments, their gardens still producing herbs for traditional local liqueurs.

Genoa's caruggi (narrow alleys) in the historic center form Europe's largest medieval quarter, where noble palaces share walls with traditional food shops selling farinata from woodfired ovens. The elevated Castelletto district, reached by historic public elevators, offers panoramic views from Liberty Style apartment buildings, while the old mariners' quarter of Boccadasse preserves its colorful fishing traditions.

In Trieste, the Habsburg quarter transports visitors to Mitteleuropa, with grand cafes where writers like James Joyce once worked. The old Jewish quarter near the grand synagogue houses bookshops in former merchant homes, while the historic Cavana district blends Roman ruins with vibrant street life.

Bergamo's Città Alta, perched above the modern city, preserves medieval life behind Venetian walls. Here, residents shop at centuries old markets and gather in squares where ancient sundials still mark time. Below, the Borgo Pignolo district showcases renaissance merchant homes with frescoed facades, their internal gardens still producing local wine.

The Parma's Oltretorrente quarter, historically home to artisans and workers, maintains its tradition of resistance and creativity. Here, traditional puppet theaters operate alongside family run tortelli shops, while the old hospital district houses recording studios in former chapel spaces with perfect acoustics.

Padua's Jewish quarter centers around the oldest active synagogue in the region, surrounded by streets where medieval bankers once lived. The Santo district, named for Saint Anthony's basilica, mixes pilgrimage traditions with university life, while the Arcella neighborhood preserves working class traditions in its community gardens and social centers.

Less obvious choices yield rich rewards. Consider Mantua's ancient pottery quarter, where artisans still work in medieval cellars, or Modena's former silkworkers' district, where traditional balsamic vinegar ages in family attics. In Ravenna's mosaic quarter, contemporary artists maintain Byzantine traditions in workshops overlooking early Christian churches.

Living like a local means embracing neighborhood rhythms – joining elderly residents for morning coffee in Turin's historic cafes, shopping at centuries old markets in Bologna's Quadrilatero, or participating in Venice's evening passeggiata along less traveled fondamente. Each quarter preserves its own traditions, from the communal bread ovens still used in mountain villages to the rooftop gardens of Milan's Brera district.

What to Pack

Packing for Northern Italy requires a thoughtful blend of practical wisdom and cultural awareness, as you'll navigate everything from cobblestone alleys to elegant opera houses, often in the same day. The region's diverse microclimates and rich cultural traditions demand a wardrobe that adapts as easily as you do.

Consider the curious case of Venice's acqua alta (high water) – while tourist shops sell disposable boots, locals carry elegant leather ones that fold into tiny pouches, perfect for unexpected flooding. These traditional boots, available from historic shoe crafters in the Castello district, double as rain gear in Milan's fashionable streets.

The mountains demand their own respect. Even summer visitors to the Dolomites should pack a wool sweater – locals swear by the traditional maglia della salute, a light undershirt that adapts to temperature changes. These garments, originally worn by mountain guides, remain popular among sophisticated Milanese for their practicality beneath business attire.

Church visits shape packing choices uniquely. Rather than carry bulky shawls, consider the pieghevole – foldable coverups sold in Venice's Jewish Quarter, originally designed for synagogue visitors but perfect for respectful tourism. Many local women carry elegant pashminas that transform from sun protection to evening wear to church appropriate covering.

The Italian approach to sun protection goes beyond basic sunscreen. Traditional widebrimmed straw hats from Florence's artisan quarter protect without wilting in sudden mountain storms. Local pharmacies sell centuriesold sunscreen formulas developed for vineyard workers, now updated with modern ingredients but still effective against the strong Alpine sun.

Footwear follows the rhythm of Italian life. While tourists wobble on cobblestones in high heels, Italians choose leather soled shoes that grip ancient pavements – many still handmade by artisans using techniques passed down through generations. Pack walking shoes with leather soles for better grip on marble steps and weathered stones.

Evening wear deserves special attention. Opera houses may no longer require gloves, but a light jacket or elegant wrap remains essential – historic theaters maintain traditional temperatures that can feel cool to modern sensibilities. Men should note that many prestigious restaurants still appreciate a jacket for dinner, though they rarely require ties.

Technology needs careful consideration. While portable chargers seem obvious, consider that many historic buildings have limited outlets – locals carry lightweight multiplugs that adapt to both ancient wiring and modern devices. A small flashlight proves invaluable in Venice's unlit calli or Turin's arcaded passages after dark.

The art of layering reaches new heights here. Mountain weather can shift dramatically, so locals practice the arte della stratificazione – the art of layering. Light wool layers work better than synthetics, allowing you to adjust comfortably from cool morning mists to warm afternoon sun. Merino wool, traditionally used by Alpine shepherds, remains popular among modern travelers for its adaptability.

For dining adventures, pack a small notebook for recording wine labels and recipe tips – many traditional restaurants don't allow photos but welcome passionate food lovers who show interest in their culinary heritage. A pocketsized Italian phrasebook earns more respect than a smartphone translator, showing consideration for local customs.

Remember the seasonal rituals. Spring travelers should pack an umbrella suited to mountain winds – locals favor models from historic makers in Milan's Brera district, designed to withstand sudden gusts. Summer visitors need protection from both sun and sudden mountain storms, while autumn demands waterproof layers that don't sacrifice style.

Swimming culture has its own rules. While beach resorts provide chairs and umbrellas, thermal spas often require swimming caps – pack one to avoid buying overpriced versions locally. Lake swimmers should bring water shoes for rocky shorelines, following a tradition dating back to Roman times.

Accessories serve multiple purposes. A good leather bag protects cameras from salt air in Venice and mountain dust in the Dolomites while meeting dress codes for elegant establishments. Traditional leather craftsmen in Florence's Santa Croce district still make bags that age beautifully while protecting their contents.

The practicalities of packing intersect with cultural respect. Light scarves serve as sun protection, evening wear, and modest covering for churches. A well chosen selection adapts to multiple situations while demonstrating cultural awareness – precisely what distinguishes thoughtful travelers from casual tourists.

Consider the unexpected. A small packet of tissue paper remains essential for churches and mountain refuges where modern amenities might be scarce. A reusable water bottle helps you take advantage of the thousands of historic fountains providing fresh Alpine water in city squares and mountain trails alike.

Entry and Visa Requirements

Entering Northern Italy connects you to centuries of traveler traditions, from medieval pilgrimage permits to modern Schengen visas. Today's requirements reflect both ancient hospitality customs and contemporary European unity, with some fascinating quirks that make the process uniquely Italian.

The Schengen visa system, which covers Northern Italy, traces its origins to an agreement signed in a tiny Luxembourg village, yet its principles echo the old Republic of Venice's pioneering role in developing diplomatic passports. For travelers needing a Schengen visa, applications go through Italy's extensive consular network, with each consulate often reflecting the architectural grandeur of Italy's diplomatic heritage – some housed in historic palazzi or modernist masterpieces.

Lesser Known entry points offer unique advantages. The SwissItalian border towns of Chiasso and Como maintain special "small border traffic permits" for regular crossers, a modern version of ancient market day passes. Similar arrangements exist in the trilingual Alto Adige region, where centuries-old mountain paths connect Italian, Austrian, and Swiss communities with special transit rights.

For nonEU visitors, Italy's permesso di soggiorno (residence permit) system reveals fascinating regional variations. Historic university cities like Bologna offer streamlined processes for scholars, maintaining a tradition from medieval times when academic freedom included special immigration status. Meanwhile, Venice's unique status as a cultural heritage site influences permit requirements for artists and restoration specialists.

Document preparation carries its own cultural nuances. While digital applications are standard, some regions still appreciate the traditional carta bollata (stamped paper) for certain declarations. In historic university towns like Padua, academic visitors might encounter the centuries old tradition of apostille certification, originally developed to authenticate scholarly credentials across medieval Europe.

Business travelers should note the peculiarities of Italy's working visa system. The prosperous northern regions maintain special quotas for skilled artisans, particularly in protected sectors like Murano glassmaking or Cremona's violin crafting. These specialized visas often come with unique requirements reflecting the historic guild systems that once governed these trades.

For those planning extended stays, the elective residence visa showcases Northern Italy's attraction for international residents since the Grand Tour era. Modern applicants often choose historic properties in regions like Lake Como or the Venetian countryside, continuing a tradition of foreign residents who have enriched local communities for centuries.

Health insurance requirements reflect both modern EU standards and Italy's historic role in developing early medical tourism. The thermal towns of the Euganean Hills, for instance, maintain special insurance arrangements dating back to when European nobility sought cures in their healing waters.

Students face an intriguing mix of ancient privilege and modern regulation. Universities like Bologna, maintaining traditions from their medieval origins, offer simplified visa processes for scholars, while specialized art academies in Venice and Florence provide unique visa categories for artists and craftspeople studying traditional techniques.

Border crossing points each tell their own story. The Alpine passes maintain centuries old customs houses, some still staffed by generations of the same families. Maritime entry through historic ports like Genoa or Venice involves procedures that echo the old maritime republics' sophisticated system of managing merchant travelers.

Digital innovation meets tradition in unexpected ways. While Italy embraces EAstandard electronic travel authorizations, some regions maintain charming anachronisms. Venice's port authority, for instance, still records arriving yachts in leatherbound registers alongside modern computer systems, continuing a practice from its seafaring golden age.

The distinction between tourist and temporary resident status reflects Italy's historic relationship with foreign visitors. The three month tourist limit echoes the traditional villeggiatura season, when nobility would retreat to countryside villas, while longer stays often required engagement with local community life, much as foreign artists and writers were once expected to contribute to cultural discourse.

Religious pilgrimage visas maintain special status, reflecting Italy's historic role in European spiritual journeys. Modern pilgrims following ancient routes like the Via Francigena can access specialized permits, while religious scholars studying in monastery libraries might qualify for particular research visas.

Understanding Italy's entry requirements means appreciating both its role in modern European unity and its rich history of managing international visitors. From the sophisticated systems of the medieval maritime republics to today's integrated EU procedures, Northern Italy's approach to welcoming travelers balances efficiency with centuries of cosmopolitan tradition.

Currency and Language

While the euro now unites Northern Italy's financial transactions, echoes of ancient currencies still influence daily life. In Venice's Rialto markets, merchants calculate prices using the traditional libbra weight system, even while charging in euros. Some mountain villages near the Swiss border still mentally convert euros to the old lira, especially among older residents discussing property values or comparing historical prices.

Local banking customs reflect centuries of financial innovation. Northern Italy, birthplace of modern banking, maintains unique traditions – some historic banks in Milan still use medieval accounting terms, while Venice's oldest banks observe customs dating from when the city standardized European currency exchange. Traditional pawn shops, the Monti di Pietà, continue operating in historic buildings, providing services much as they did when they were founded to combat usury in the Renaissance.

The language landscape reveals fascinating layers of history and culture. While Italian predominates, each region preserves its distinct linguistic heritage. In the valleys of the Dolomites, Ladin survives as a living link to Roman times, used not just for folklore but in modern business and education. The Walser communities near Monte Rosa maintain their medieval German dialect, once used by traveling merchants crossing the Alps.

Venice's maritime heritage lives on in its vocabulary – modern water taxi drivers use nautical terms that haven't changed since the Republic's golden age. Local newspapers still print tide times using traditional

Venetian measurements, while fishmongers call out their wares in dialect names that would have been familiar to Marco Polo.

In Milan's financial district, a curious blend of ancient and modern terminology thrives. Stockbrokers mix English financial jargon with traditional Lombard trading terms, while historic textile merchants in Como still use silk trading vocabulary from the Middle Ages. The city's commodity exchange preserves pricing units that date back to medieval fairs.

Mountain communities maintain their own linguistic ecosystems. The Occitan valleys of Piedmont preserve a language once used by troubadours, now adapted for modern communication while maintaining ancient terms for weather patterns and agricultural techniques. In Alto Adige, three official languages – Italian, German, and Ladin – coexist in a sophisticated system that ensures every official document and street sign reflects this unique heritage.

Banking hours follow traditional rhythms that vary by region. In the Po Valley, some rural banks still observe the old agricultural calendar, while coastal towns maintain banking schedules that once accommodated maritime trade. Modern ATMs in historic centers often occupy the same niches where medieval money changers once conducted business.

The tradition of contrattazione (negotiation) survives in market towns, where bargaining follows unwritten rules passed down through generations. In artisanal workshops, pricing often involves traditional measurements – Murano glassmakers quote weights in traditional Venetian ounces, while Cremona's violin makers discuss wood quantities using ancient Lombardy units.

Local expressions reveal economic history. Venetians still say "non vale un bagattino" (not worth a bagattino) referring to their smallest medieval coin, while Genoese use "vale un Peru" (worth a Peru) from their days financing Spanish colonial trade. Traditional markets in Bologna sometimes reference weights and measures established by medieval guild statutes.

Digital payments merge with historical practice in unexpected ways. Some historic cafes in Turin's porticoed streets maintain accounts for regular customers following a system established in the 18th century, now adapted to electronic payments. Venice's traghetti (gondola crossings) accept contactless payments while charging fares calculated using traditional fare zones.

Language preservation efforts take innovative forms. Milan's fashion district maintains specialized vocabulary for textile qualities that dates back centuries, now used alongside modern technical terms. Traditional craftspeople in Murano pass down secret glassmaking terminology through apprenticeships, preserving words that exist nowhere else.

Financial customs reflect regional character. The Piedmontese reputation for fiscal prudence influences modern banking practices, while Venetian banks maintain sophisticated foreign exchange services rooted in their trading history. Some mountain communities preserve collective banking traditions that echo medieval Alpine cooperatives.

Understanding currency and language here means appreciating living history. A conversation with a local shopkeeper might blend standard Italian with dialect terms for traditional products, while a restaurant bill might arrive calculated in modern euros but presented with traditional

Venetian flourishes. This layering of old and new creates a unique linguistic and financial landscape where history remains very much alive.

Suggested Budget

Budgeting for Northern Italy involves understanding the subtle rhythms of local economics, where ancient traditions influence modern spending patterns. Your daily expenses dance to the tune of regional customs, seasonal celebrations, and centuries old market practices that still shape today's costs.

In Venice, early morning explorers discover the traditional bacari serve cicchetti (small bites) at prices that haven't changed much since the days of the Republic – €1.50 for classic baccalà mantecato on polenta, while coffee at historic counter prices (€1.20 standing) reflects old guild regulations designed to keep morning rituals affordable. Meanwhile, afternoon spreads to early evening aperitivo culture, where €1215 buys drinks and substantial buffets in Milan's Navigli district.

Mountain economies follow their own rules. Alpine rifugi (mountain huts) maintain traditional halfpension rates (€4560) that include dinner, bed, and breakfast, following pricing customs established by early climbing societies. In the Dolomites, the "Alpine breakfast" (€812) offers extraordinary value, as farming families serve homemade cheeses and preserves following age old hospitality traditions.

Cultural experiences reveal fascinating price variations. While top venues command premium prices, many historic theaters offer traditional "loggione" tickets (€1525) in upper galleries, continuing a custom that once made opera accessible to artisans and students. Sunday morning concert aperitivi in historic palazzos (€2030) include both culture and sustenance, reviving an aristocratic tradition in accessible form.

Accommodation costs reflect architectural heritage. In Venice, rooms in converted merchants' houses (€80120) often offer better value than modern hotels, while monasteries turned guesthouses maintain modest pricing (€5070) following centuries old hospitality traditions. Milan's historic case di ringhiera (traditional apartment buildings) now offer rooms through resident associations (€6590), providing authentic experiences at reasonable costs.

Dining budgets follow daily rhythms. Worker's cafes in Turin's historic center still serve traditional three course pranzo di lavoro (worker's lunch) for €1215, while evening meals see wider price ranges. Traditional osterie in Bologna's university quarter maintain student friendly pricing (€2535 for full meals), a custom dating back to medieval times when the university regulated local food costs.

Transportation costs benefit from regional passes reflecting historical trade routes. The Alto Adige museum pass (€30 for 3 days) covers transport and culture in an area once united under Habsburg rule, while Venice's vaporetto passes follow traditional fare zones established during the Republic.

For self catering, local markets reveal budget friendly secrets. Morning markets in Milan's working class quarters maintain traditional "last hour" discounts (up to 50% off), while Venice's Rialto markets observe ancient customs of reducing prices for less perfect but perfectly good produce. Traditional bread shops in Turin still offer day old grissini and breadsticks at heritage prices.

Seasonal variations significantly impact budgets. During sagre (food festivals), entire villages offer setprice feasts (€2030) celebrating local specialties, while winter in the Alps brings traditional ski week

49

packages following models established in the 1930s tourism boom. Religious festivals often mean free cultural events and community meals, continuing medieval traditions of public celebration.

Shopping wisely means understanding local patterns. Historic artisan quarters in cities like Florence and Venice maintain "workshop direct" pricing for leather goods and glass, while outlet villages near Milan offer Italian luxury goods at 3070% off through traditional stock clearance systems.

Art appreciation needn't strain budgets. Many churches housing masterpieces remain free, while civic museums often maintain "citizens' hours" with reduced entry fees, a tradition dating from when aristocratic collections were first opened to the public. State museums offer free entry on first Sundays, continuing Italy's commitment to cultural accessibility.

Weekly budgets vary by approach:
   Essential Experience: €7090/day covers basic comfortable accommodation, local transport, and meals at traditional establishments
   Classic Comfort: €120150/day allows for better located hotels, occasional fine dining, and regular cultural activities
   Heritage Experience: €200250/day opens doors to historic properties, finest restaurants, and exclusive cultural events

Practical touches reflect regional character. Northern Italian cities maintain networks of public water fountains providing free Alpine water, while traditional bars serve complimentary snacks with evening drinks, reflecting ancient hospitality customs. University cities preserve student friendly pricing in historic cafes and trattorias, maintaining centuries old relationships between towns and scholars.

Understanding these patterns helps create both memorable experiences and reasonable budgets. By aligning your spending with local rhythms – morning markets, aperitivo culture, festival celebrations – you'll discover how Northern Italy's sophisticated culture remains surprisingly accessible, guided by traditions that have balanced quality and value for centuries.

MoneySaving Tips

Northern Italy's sophisticated culture of elegance and artistry doesn't demand a fortune when you understand local wisdom about living well while spending wisely. Centuries of merchant traditions and community practices have created unique opportunities for experiencing luxury at surprisingly accessible prices.

Secret kitchen tables flourish in Bologna's historic center, where home cooks maintain the medieval tradition of "cucina nascosta" (hidden kitchen). These invitation-only dining rooms, often in centuries old apartments, offer multicourse feasts for €2535, continuing a custom that once fed traveling scholars. Connect through local food markets or neighborhood associations to discover these authentic experiences.

Venice's traditional craftspeople often welcome visitors to their workshops during restoration hours (typically 35 PM), when they practice new techniques on practice pieces. You might watch master glass bead makers or mask artisans at work, gaining insights typically reserved for expensive tours. Some workshops even sell these practice pieces at fraction of normal prices.

University cities maintain charming academic traditions that visitors can access. In Padua, joining informal "library tours" with art history students provides free access to frescoed halls normally closed to tourists. Bologna's historic student associations occasionally open their centuries old dining halls to visitors, offering three course meals at student prices (€1215).

Mountain communities preserve money saving customs from ancient times. The Alto Adige's "alpine summer" program lets visitors join traditional hay making activities in exchange for meals and mountain hut accommodation. Similar arrangements exist throughout the Dolomites, where farming families maintain the tradition of exchanging work for hospitality.

Religious houses across Northern Italy continue their historic mission of hospitality. Beyond well known monastery stays, some communities offer unique experiences – join Benedictine monks in Piedmont for grape harvesting (free accommodation plus wine), or help Franciscan friars tend historic herb gardens in exchange for lodging and botanical wisdom.

Train travel becomes remarkably affordable through regional passes that follow ancient pilgrimage routes. The "Via Francigena" pass combines transport with monastery stays and local experiences, while some mountain trains offer special rates for early morning "workers'" trains – originally designed for factory workers but perfect for early rising tourists.

Venice's traditional traghetti (gondola crossings) cost just €2 standing, compared to €80+ for tourist gondola rides. These crossing points have operated since the Republic's days, offering the authentic gondola experience as locals use it. Similarly, joining early morning cargo deliveries by boat can provide free canal tours while experiencing the city's working life.

Historic markets follow ancient timing traditions that create natural discounts. The last hour at Turin's Porta Palazzo market sees prices drop by half, following customs established when workers would shop after factory shifts. Similarly, Monday mornings offer special prices as vendors clear weekend stock, a practice dating to medieval market regulations.

Cultural access comes surprisingly cheap through traditional community practices. Many historic palazzos in Milan open their courtyards for free classical concerts during lunch hours, maintaining an aristocratic tradition of public patronage. Venice's churches host free evening vespers concerts, often featuring world class musicians practicing for major performances.

Aperitivo culture provides exceptional value when you know local customs. Historic bars in Turin's porticoed streets serve traditional "merenda sinoira" (afternoon meal) with drinks, following a custom that began when factory workers needed substantial snacks between shifts. Modern venues maintain this tradition with elaborate buffets included in drink prices (€1012).

Seasonal festivals offer immersive experiences at minimal cost. During traditional sagre (food festivals), entire villages become open air dining rooms with setprice feasts celebrating local specialties. Religious celebrations often mean free access to historic buildings normally closed to visitors, plus community meals and cultural performances.

Art viewing becomes accessible through traditional "artists' hours" – many historic cafes and restaurants display rotating exhibitions where purchasing a coffee (€1.201.50) grants you time to appreciate original artworks. Similarly, contemporary galleries in historic districts often host free vernissage evenings with prosecco and appetizers.

Lesser Known transport passes unlock significant savings. The "Industrial Heritage" card in Turin includes transport and entry to converted factory museums, while Venice's "Chorus Pass" combines vaporetto travel with church visits following traditional pilgrim routes.

Living like a local reveals natural economies. Shopping at traditional markets usually halves food costs compared to supermarkets, while joining neighborhood wine cooperatives provides access to quality wines at producer prices. Many historic districts maintain community dining rooms where residents share costs for traditional group meals, often welcoming visitors who learn about these options through local contacts.

Best Places to Book Your Trip

Northern Italy's rich tapestry of experiences becomes even more accessible when you know where to look beyond the obvious booking platforms. Local cultural associations, historic institutions, and traditional hospitality networks often offer unique opportunities that major travel sites miss entirely.

The Touring Club Italiano, founded in 1894, maintains special relationships with historic properties throughout Northern Italy. Their members only booking platform (membership costs €68 annually) unlocks access to restored monasteries, noble villas, and authentic agriturismi that rarely appear on mainstream sites. Many of these properties maintain traditional hospitality practices, from seasonal wine tastings to truffle hunting experiences.

Venice's traditional Associazione Veneziana Albergatori operates a lesser known booking service specializing in authentic family run properties. Through their platform, you can find rooms in historic palazzi where current owners maintain portions of their ancestral homes as guesthouses, offering intimate glimpses into Venetian life rarely experienced by regular tourists.

For mountain experiences, the Club Alpino Italiano's refuge booking system connects travelers with historic mountain huts, many dating from the 19th century. Their network includes former royal hunting lodges, restored shepherds' huts, and traditional alpine chalets, many offering halfboard arrangements that include traditional mountain cuisine.

Local agricultural consortiums throughout the Po Valley maintain booking systems for agriturismi that participate in traditional farming activities. These platforms often include detailed information about seasonal activities – from rice harvesting to cheesemaking – allowing visitors to plan stays around authentic agricultural experiences.

The Associazione Dimore Storiche Italiane coordinates bookings for historic homes across Northern Italy. Their members open private wings of ancestral palaces, converted stable blocks, and restored watermills for overnight stays. Many properties maintain original furnishings and offer unique experiences like dining in frescoed halls or exploring historic gardens.

University cities like Bologna, Padua, and Pavia maintain accommodation offices that coordinate stays in historic college buildings during academic holidays. Some colleges occupy former monasteries or noble palaces, offering simple but atmospheric rooms at reasonable rates, often including access to historic libraries or gardens.

Regional wine consortiums operate booking platforms connecting visitors with traditional wine estates. Many properties offer accommodation in converted farmhouses or renovated workers' quarters, often including cellar tours and tastings. Some maintain historic traditions like seasonal grape harvesting experiences or traditional feast day celebrations.

The Slow Food movement, born in Piedmont, coordinates bookings through local chapters for properties committed to traditional gastronomy. Their network includes historic inns, working farms, and familyrun hotels where traditional cooking methods and local ingredients take center stage.

For cultural experiences, regional theater foundations maintain booking systems for performance packages that include accommodation in historic properties. These often combine opera tickets with stays in buildings connected to famous composers or performers, creating uniquely immersive cultural experiences.

Historic craft guilds in cities like Venice and Florence coordinate specialized stays focused on traditional artisanal practices. These might include accommodation in workshopsturnedguesthouses or arrangements combining lodging with craft demonstrations or handson experiences.

Religious hospitality networks continue centuriesold traditions of pilgrim accommodation. Many monasteries and convents maintain online booking systems offering simple but atmospheric rooms, often including traditional meals and opportunities to participate in community life.

The Confederazione Nazionale dell'Artigianato coordinates stays with artisan families throughout Northern Italy. Their booking platform connects travelers with craftspeople who maintain guest rooms, offering unique opportunities to experience traditional crafts firsthand while staying in authentic workshops or historic artisan quarters.

Local cultural associations in smaller cities often maintain accommodation booking services focusing on properties connected to specific historical periods or cultural movements. These might include art nouveau villas in Turin, rationalist apartments in Como, or medieval tower houses in Bologna.

Regional park authorities coordinate bookings for unique properties within protected areas. Options might include restored forestry stations, converted lighthouse keepers' cottages, or traditional alpine dairy farms, many maintaining historical functions alongside visitor accommodation.

Professional guilds occasionally open their historic headquarters for special stays. The ancient universities' medical, legal, and mercantile guilds maintain guest quarters in historic buildings, often available through direct booking with the institutions.

Traditional hamams and historic spa towns maintain booking systems for properties connected to thermal waters. Some continue centuriesold practices of health tourism, combining accommodation with traditional treatments in historic bathing establishments.

For railway enthusiasts, the Ferrovie dello Stato occasionally offers stays in converted station buildings and signal boxes along scenic routes. These unique properties, often in spectacular locations, provide atmospheric accommodation while preserving railway heritage.

Maritime museums along the coast coordinate stays in restored historic vessels, from traditional fishing boats to converted cargo ships. These floating accommodations often maintain original features while providing unique perspectives on historic ports.

Remember that many of these specialized booking channels require advance planning and sometimes direct communication in Italian. However, they often reward the extra effort with extraordinary experiences and better value than mainstream options, while supporting the preservation of Northern Italy's rich cultural heritage.

CHAPTER 2: MUST SEE ATTRACTIONS AND LANDMARKS

From the dramatic peaks of the Dolomites to the romantic waterways of Venice's Grand Canal, Northern Italy's landmarks paint a mesmerizing portrait of natural and architectural splendor. These UNESCOlisted mountains share the spotlight with the glittering waters of Lake Como, where elegant villas peek through cypress trees, while the candy colored houses of Cinque Terre tumble down to meet the Mediterranean Sea. Meanwhile, Milan's Gothic cathedral pierces the sky with its forest of spires, its marble facade telling stories in stone just as Verona's ancient arena resonates with the echoes of centuries of performance and passion.

The picture perfect harbor of Portofino, with its jewel colored houses embracing the sea, captures the same timeless beauty that draws visitors to Pisa's magnificent Campo dei Miracoli, where the famous Leaning Tower stands among a collection of masterpieces in marble. These architectural wonders find their match in Parma's intricately decorated Baptistery, where medieval artisans left their mark in stone and fresco, creating a symphony of color and form that still captivates visitors today.

In the embrace of the Italian Alps, the Aosta Valley unfolds like a storybook of medieval castles and Roman ruins, where ancient paths wind through valleys once walked by Celtic tribes and Roman legions. This remarkable landscape completes a journey through Northern Italy that weaves together soaring mountains and serene waters, timeless villages and magnificent cities, each destination adding its own chapter to a story that spans millennia of human creativity and natural wonder.

The Dolomites

The Dolomites whisper secrets of ancient seas – these majestic peaks were once coral reefs thrust skyward by tectonic forces 250 million years ago. Their unique mineral composition of magnesium and calcium carbonate creates the distinctive enrosadira effect, painting the mountains in shades of pink and violet at dawn and dusk, a phenomenon that has inspired countless legends among local Ladin communities.

Hidden in these valleys, the Ladin people maintain Europe's oldest mountain culture, speaking a language that preserves traces of preRoman times. Their traditional wooden homes, called tabià, feature distinctive carved balconies where generations have dried herbs and hay, while ancient sundials on church towers still accurately mark time using shadow patterns understood by medieval astronomers.

The mountains harbor extraordinary biological treasures – the Dolomites host 1,700 plant species, including the rare Dolomite Moon Flower that blooms only one night each year. Alpine meadows called "malghe" preserve unique ecosystems where farmers still practice transhumance, moving cattle between altitudes following cycles established in prehistoric times. These seasonal migrations maintain biodiversity patterns crucial for endemic butterfly species found nowhere else on Earth.

Traditional mountain huts, or rifugi, each tell their own story. The Rifugio Nuvolau, perched at 2,575 meters, began as a military observatory in 1883 and now serves traditional dishes using preservation methods developed by early mountaineers. Some rifugi maintain libraries of Alpine literature and journals dating back to the first scientific expeditions, while others preserve collections of minerals discovered during World War I trench digging.

The region's via ferrata network originated not from tourism but necessity – local mountain guides installed the first iron cables and ladders to help crystal hunters access remote peaks where they searched for the perfect "Enrosadira quartz," believed to capture the mountains' pink glow. Today, over 600 equipped routes trace paths first mapped by these mineral seekers and later used by military troops during World War I.

Water shapes these mountains in unexpected ways. The distinctive "earth pyramids" near Bolzano form when rainwater erodes soft clay soil while leaving stones atop natural pillars, creating formations that local folklore attributes to mountain spirits. Underground, vast cave systems carved by ancient glaciers preserve ice formations that scientists use to study climate patterns dating back 150,000 years.

Traditional crafts reflect the mountains' mineral wealth. The art of intarsia (wood inlay) in Val Gardena developed using 13 different native wood species, each chosen for its unique grain pattern. Local artisans still create traditional masks for Krampus ceremonies using stone pigments gathered from specific mountain faces, following color recipes passed down through generations.

Mountain agriculture follows vertical patterns unique to the Dolomites. Vineyards at 1,000 meters produce distinctive wines from grapes adapted to extreme altitudes, while ancient grain varieties like "Regiokorn" survive in high valleys where modern crops won't grow. Some mountain communities maintain communal bread ovens that operate only five times yearly, following a medieval schedule aligned with pastoral festivals.

The mountains influence local cuisine in fascinating ways. Traditional dishes like canederli (bread dumplings) vary their ingredients by altitude – incorporating wild herbs above 1,500 meters and preserved meats at lower elevations. Some rifugi still age cheese in natural caves where specific air currents create conditions impossible to replicate elsewhere.

Sound travels mysteriously here – certain valleys are known for their perfect acoustics, used for centuries by shepherds to communicate across distances. The phenomenon of "mountain sound" occurs when specific temperature conditions create natural amplification, allowing whispers to carry for kilometers through certain passes.

Weather patterns create unique microclimates. The "föhn" wind phenomenon can raise valley temperatures by 10°C in hours, while some high meadows experience their own cloud systems independent of surrounding weather. Traditional weather predictors still watch for signs like the formation of specific cloud shapes above certain peaks, using knowledge accumulated over centuries.

Modern conservation efforts blend with ancient practices. The traditional Ladin system of "regole" (community land management) proves remarkably effective at preserving biodiversity, while contemporary biologists study how historical grazing patterns maintain crucial habitats for endangered species like the bearded vulture.

Recent discoveries continue to reveal new wonders. Melting glaciers expose dinosaur tracks and fossilized tropical plants, while acoustic studies reveal how the mountains' unique mineral composition creates natural resonance chambers used in traditional alpine singing. Each season brings new understanding of these remarkable peaks, where nature and human history intertwine in ever surprising ways.

Lake Como

Location: Lombardy Region, Northern Italy
Coordinates: 45°59′N 9°15′E
Distance from Milan: 50 kilometers (31 miles)
Nearest Airports: Milan Malpensa (MXP) and Milan Linate (LIN)

Lake Como's distinctive Shape wasn't formed by chance – it follows ancient fault lines carved by glaciers during the last Ice Age, creating one of the deepest lakes in Europe at 425 meters. Local fishermen still refer to these depths as "the mountains underwater," where unique freshwater fish species thrive in pressure conditions similar to deep ocean environments.

The lake's mysterious currents, called "lumaghitt" by locals, create natural thermoclines that allow Mediterranean plants to flourish at unusually northern latitudes. Ancient Roman aristocrats discovered these microclimates, establishing the world's first cultivated olive groves north of the 46th parallel. These same groves still produce oil today, with some trees dating back over 1,000 years.

Hidden beneath the surface lies a network of underwater springs called "sortive," which local fishermen have mapped through generations. These springs influence water temperature and fish behavior, creating unique fishing zones that follow patterns first documented by Celtic tribes. The lake's depth and these springs maintain a constant water temperature of 6°C at the bottom, preserving ancient shipwrecks in remarkable condition.

The lake's traditional boats tell stories of evolving craftsmanship. The Lucia, a distinctive flatbottomed vessel, was designed specifically for Como's wind patterns and shallow coastal waters. Local boatyards still build these craft using techniques passed down through generations, selecting wood based on the moon's phases – a practice scientific studies have shown affects timber density.

Historic gardens along the shore preserve rare botanical treasures. Villa Carlotta's citrus collection includes varieties brought by the Crusaders, while Villa Melzi maintains azalea species thought extinct elsewhere. The traditional art of lakeside gardening, called "giardinaggio lariano," involves unique pruning techniques developed to work with the lake's reflected light.

The lake's silkmaking heritage remains alive in unexpected ways. Historic mulberry groves on terraced hillsides still support smallscale silk production, while former silkspinning mills now house artisan workshops. Some villas maintain "silk rooms" where specific temperature and humidity conditions, created by the lake's influence, made perfect silk storage possible.

Local architecture responds uniquely to the environment. Traditional lake houses feature "ventane," special window systems that use lake breezes for natural cooling. Historic villas were built with "limonaie" – citrus houses with removable glass panels that could be adjusted to protect delicate plants while maximizing lake views.

The lake's influence on local cuisine extends beyond fish. Mountain herbs growing at specific altitudes above the lake are essential ingredients in traditional dishes, while the unique moisture patterns create perfect conditions for aging cheese in lakeside caves. Some restaurants maintain floating vegetable gardens, reviving a practice from medieval times when fresh produce was grown on rafts.

Weather phenomena here fascinate meteorologists. The "Tivano" and "Breva" winds follow such reliable daily patterns that historic boat schedules were built around them. The lake creates its own microclimate, with distinct weather systems that can differ dramatically from conditions just kilometers away. Local farmers still consult traditional wind calendars for planting, following patterns first recorded by Leonardo da Vinci during his studies of the lake.

Cultural traditions unique to Como persist in daily life. The "Lucia" celebration in December features floating lights that follow ancient fishermen's routes, while summer's "Sagra di San Giovanni" includes a water procession using boats decorated according to centuriesold protocols. Some villages maintain traditional signaling systems using bells and flags, once used to communicate weather warnings across the lake.

Modern life adapts to ancient rhythms here. Solarpowered water taxis follow routes established by Roman galleys, while lakeside markets still operate on schedules tied to historic fishing patterns. Contemporary architects studying the lake's traditional buildings discover sophisticated passive cooling systems that inspire sustainable design solutions.

Recent archaeological discoveries continue to reveal new chapters in Como's story. Underwater surveys have found evidence of prehistoric stilt houses, while renovation works occasionally uncover Roman artifacts in lakeside gardens. Each finding adds to our understanding of how humans have interacted with this remarkable body of water across millennia, creating a living laboratory of natural and cultural history.

Cinque Terre

Location: Liguria Region, Northern Italy
Cinque Terre comprises five picturesque villages: Monterosso al Mare, Vernazza, Corniglia, Manarola, and Riomaggiore.
Province: La Spezia
Coordinates: 44°08′N 9°43′E
Nearest Airports: Pisa International Airport (PSA) and Genoa Cristoforo Colombo Airport (GOA)

Cinque Terre's dramatic terraces hold secrets of medieval engineering – their distinctive dry stone walls, called "muretti a secco," extend for an astonishing 6,729 kilometers, longer than the Great Wall of China if laid end to end. These walls, built without mortar, use an ancient technique that allows them to flex during earthquakes while channeling water to prevent landslides. Each stone's placement follows patterns first developed by Benedictine monks in the 11th century.

The region's unique microclimate creates unexpected agricultural treasures. The rare Bosco variety of grape grows nowhere else in the world, thriving in salty sea breezes that other vines can't tolerate. Local winemakers still use ancient stone monorails called "monorotaie" to transport grapes down precipitous slopes, some operating on counterweight systems designed during the Renaissance.

Hidden beneath the colorful houses lies a network of medieval water management systems. Each village maintains its own historic cistern network, with some still using original Romanera filters made from local stone. The village of Corniglia's elevated position resulted in an ingenious medieval hydraulic system that used gravity and ceramic pipes to distribute water – parts of this system remain functional today.

The villages' distinctive colors emerged from practical necessity. Fishermen painted their houses in bright hues visible from sea, creating a natural navigation system. Each family's traditional color combinations were registered in town records, some dating back to the 14th century. These chromatic codes also helped sailors identify their homes during storms, with specific color patterns indicating family allegiances and maritime professions.

Local cuisine reflects centuries of isolation. The unique anchovy preserving technique of Monterosso, recognized by Slow Food, uses local salt and specific wooden barrels made from chestnut trees grown at exact altitudes. Traditional pasta shapes like "croxetti" bear family stamps that once served as currency among villagers during times of economic hardship.

The area's botanical heritage surprises scientists. Isolated patches between terraces harbor plant species believed extinct elsewhere in Europe, while some olive trees show genetic markers traceable to Greek colonists. Local herbalists maintain knowledge of medicinal plants that grow only on specific terraces, their properties first documented by medieval monasteries.

Maritime traditions here differ from elsewhere along the Italian coast. The unique "gozzo" fishing boats of Cinque Terre feature asymmetrical designs adapted to the region's particular wave patterns and rocky coves. Local fishermen still practice the ancient art of "lampara" night fishing, using light to attract fish – a technique that requires understanding complex lunar and tidal interactions.

Each village preserves distinct cultural practices. Manarola's Christmas illumination tradition began as a fisherman's tribute using recycled maritime materials. Vernazza maintains Europe's smallest natural port, where ancient mooring techniques use underwater rock formations mapped by generations of sailors. Riomaggiore's historic cooperatives still operate on medieval bylaws that ensure sustainable fishing practices.

The famous pathways between villages tell stories beyond tourism. The Via dell'Amore originally served as a meeting point for young couples from Riomaggiore and Manarola when the villages were rivals. Other paths follow routes first mapped by salt traders, with historic rest stops carved into cliff faces still visible today.

Traditional farming practices preserve crucial biodiversity. The steep terraces create numerous microclimates within meters of each other, supporting different species. Local farmers still practice companion planting techniques developed through centuries of trial and error, documented in family journals passed down through generations.

Recent archaeological discoveries reveal new layers of history. Underwater surveys have found evidence of Roman fish farms near Monterosso, while renovation work occasionally uncovers medieval frescos preserved by the region's unique mineralrich atmosphere. Scientists study how the terraces' stone composition affects soil chemistry, creating distinctive growing conditions for local wine varieties.

Modern conservation efforts blend technology with tradition. Drone surveys help maintain the ancient walls using traditional techniques, while seismic monitoring stations study how the historic engineering continues to protect against landslides. Some terraces now incorporate subtle modern reinforcement while maintaining their original water management capabilities.

The future of Cinque Terre balances preservation with innovation. Local initiatives use historic agricultural techniques to combat climate change effects, while traditional weather prediction methods, based on generations of observation, help inform modern meteorological studies. Each village continues to evolve while maintaining its distinct character, creating a living laboratory of sustainable coastal living.

Venice and its Grand Canal

Location: Veneto Region, Northern Italy
Setting: Venetian Lagoon
Coordinates: 45°26′N 12°20′E
Nearest Airport: Marco Polo International Airport (VCE)
Distance from mainland: 4 kilometers

The Grand Canal's distinctive Shape follows the course of an ancient river, its curves carefully engineered during the 8th century to slow water flow and prevent erosion. This serpentine waterway, called "Canalazzo" by locals, maintains a complex ecosystem were twice daily tidal flows help naturally clean the city – a sophisticated system first designed by hydraulic engineers in the Republic's golden age.

Beneath the water's surface lies an engineering marvel – the canal rests on millions of wooden piles driven into the clay seabed. These piles, cut from special forests in the Dolomites during specific moon phases, have petrified over centuries due to unique mineral conditions in the lagoon. Some date back to the 9th century, their wood harder than steel due to underwater mineralization.

The palaces along the canal tell stories through their foundations. Each noble family developed unique techniques for building on water – some palazzos float on thousands of pine logs, while others use innovative stoneandwood combinations that flex with the tides. Recent radar surveys have revealed hidden internal canals within some buildings, once used for secret maritime trade.

Traditional Venetian measurement systems still influence modern life. Water levels are marked using ancient "piedi veneti" (Venetian feet) scales carved into palace walls, while boat speeds follow patterns established when gondoliers first standardized rowing techniques in the 14th century. Some bridges maintain medieval tide markers that local fishermen still consult.

The canal's acoustics create fascinating phenomena. Certain points along its course amplify sounds in ways that gondoliers once used for communication. Early morning water traffic still follows routes designed to minimize sound reflection between buildings – patterns first established when Venice regulated noise pollution in the 15th century.

Hidden gardens flourish behind palace walls, maintaining centuriesold horticultural traditions. Some courtyard gardens use sophisticated medieval irrigation systems that filter salt from lagoon water, while others preserve rare plant species brought by merchant ships during the Republic's trading days. Ancient fig trees grow from walls where their roots help stabilize foundations.

Maritime traditions shape daily life in unexpected ways. Traditional cargo boats still use measuring systems based on the "staro veneziano," a volume unit from the Republic era. Modern water taxis follow lanes established by medieval maritime laws, while some delivery services use restored traditional boats designed for specific cargo types.

The canal's unique ecosystem supports surprising biodiversity. Small crabs that live in palace walls play crucial roles in preventing erosion, while certain algae species, first documented by 18th century naturalists, help clean the water naturally. Recent studies have identified microorganisms unique to Venice's waterways that contribute to the preservation of underwater wooden structures.

Architectural details serve practical purposes beyond decoration. The distinctive chimney pots (fumaioli) on palace roofs were designed to cope with lagoon winds, while ornate wellheads in courtyards connect to sophisticated rainwater filtering systems. Even decorative elements on facades often functioned as medieval tide indicators or wind markers.

Traditional crafts adapt to water based life. Glass makers from Murano developed special techniques for creating windows that flex with building movement, while wood carvers still use ancient methods to craft boat components that resist salt water. Some workshops maintain Byzantine Era techniques for waterproofing textiles using local minerals.

Modern conservation efforts reveal historical ingenuity. Scientists studying palace foundations have discovered that medieval builders created "sacrificial" lower floors designed to manage flooding while protecting upper levels. Contemporary architects now incorporate these principles into restoration projects.

The canal's relationship with art continues to evolve. Modern artists study how centuries of boat wakes have sculpted marble steps, creating unique patterns that influence contemporary designs. Some palaces maintain original color schemes made from ground minerals and lagoon algae, pigments that scientists are now analyzing for their durability.

Local knowledge about the canal's behavior passes through generations. Boat operators understand complex wave patterns caused by building reflections, while residents recognize subtle water color changes that indicate tidal shifts. This practical wisdom, combined with modern technology, helps maintain this extraordinary waterway's delicate balance.

Climate change brings new challenges to ancient solutions. Venice now combines traditional water management techniques with innovative technology, while studying how historical engineering might help address rising sea levels. Each intervention must respect the delicate ecosystem that has evolved over a millennium of human interaction with this remarkable waterway.

Verona Arena

Location: Piazza Bra, Verona, Veneto Region
Coordinates: 45°26'20"N 10°59'38"E
Nearest Airports: Valerio Catullo Airport (VRN) and Marco Polo Airport (VCE)
Built: 30 AD

Verona Arena's pink limestone holds acoustic secrets that modern engineers still struggle to understand. The amphitheater's perfect sound distribution allows whispers from the arena floor to reach the highest tier – achieved through precise mathematical ratios in its construction that create natural amplification. Recent studies reveal how ancient architects used specific stone cuts to enhance frequencies matching the human voice.

The arena's original seating system employed sophisticated crowd management techniques. Numbered archways corresponded to specific social classes, while ingeniously designed stairways prevented bottlenecks by following mathematical progressions that spatially distributed crowds. Modern sporting venues still study these ancient crowdflow patterns.

Underground, a complex network of tunnels reveals revolutionary engineering. The hypogeum (underground area) featured mechanical lifts powered by counterweights, allowing scenery and gladiators to appear seemingly from nowhere. Some of these lifting mechanisms used bronze bushings so precisely engineered that modern replicas require computer guided manufacturing to achieve similar tolerances.

The arena's stone tells geological stories. Its distinctive pink Valpolicella marble contains fossils visible in worn steps, while different colored stone bands mark construction phases spanning several emperors' reigns. Each restoration project discovers new mason's marks, ancient quality control systems that tracked which craftsman cut each block.

Summer opera productions here maintain traditions dating to 1913, but the arena's acoustic properties follow principles first established for Roman military signals. Specific points in the structure create standing wave patterns that amplifiers now use to enhance natural acoustics. Orchestra conductors learn secret positions marked by worn spots in the marble where sound projection reaches its peak.

The arena's survival through earthquakes reveals sophisticated antiseismic engineering. Its elliptical shape and precisely angled stone blocks dissipate seismic waves, while flexible mortar joints allow minimal movement during tremors. Modern architects study how these ancient techniques outperform some contemporary earthquake resistant designs.

Hidden water management systems showcase Roman ingenuity. Channels carved into stairs doubled as drainage systems during rain, while underground cisterns collected water for staging mock naval battles. Some original bronze drainage pipes still function, their unique alloy composition protecting against corrosion for two millennia.

The arena's role in medieval Verona extended beyond entertainment. During plague outbreaks, its excellent ventilation and separated seating sections served public health functions. The structure also preserved ancient mathematical knowledge – its proportions were studied by Renaissance architects rediscovering classical geometry.

Conservation efforts reveal fascinating details about Roman construction techniques. Recent radar surveys showed how builders used lead plates between stone blocks to distribute weight evenly, while metallic pins connecting blocks were positioned according to astronomical alignments. Some original wooden beams survive, preserved by mineral deposits from centuries of seepage.

The venue's lighting system tells its own story. Original torch brackets remain visible, positioned to maximize illumination while minimizing smoke accumulation. Modern lighting designers discovered that these ancient positions create optimal atmospheric effects for contemporary performances.

Climate monitoring stations throughout the structure help conservators understand how the arena breathes. Different sections maintain distinct microclimates, with air circulation patterns that change seasonally. These variations, first noted in Roman times, influenced seating arrangements for different times of year.

Archaeological work continues revealing new chapters in the arena's story. Ground Penetrating radar recently discovered previously unknown chambers, while analysis of mortar samples provides insights into Roman concrete technology. Each discovery adds to our understanding of this remarkable structure where engineering genius meets theatrical magic.

The arena's future brings new challenges. Conservation teams now use 3D modeling to understand stress patterns in the ancient stone, while developing techniques to protect the structure from modern air pollution. Yet the building continues serving its original purpose –

bringing people together for spectacular performances, just as it has for nearly two thousand years.

Milan Cathedral (Duomo di Milano)

Location: Piazza del Duomo, 20122 Milan
Coordinates: 45°27′51″N 9°11′29″E
Nearest Airports: Milan Malpensa (MXP) and Milan Linate (LIN)
Construction Period: 13861965

The Duomo's forest of spires conceals an intricate water collection system – each of its 135 pinnacles doubles as a sophisticated drainage channel, Hidden cisterns, which once supplied the city's medieval water system, were fed by rainwater that was directed through gargoyle mouths. These architectural marvels use pressure differentials and gravity to prevent marble erosion while managing Milan's notorious rainfall.

Behind the cathedral's gleaming façade lies an engineering secret – the entire structure rests on wooden foundations submerged in underground canals. These ancient waterways, part of Milan's medieval canal system, keep the wood permanently wet, preventing decay through a process that petrifies the timber into stone-like hardness. Regular monitoring reveals these 600 year old foundations remain structurally sound.

The Duomo's marble tells a remarkable geological story. Quarried from special caves near Lake Maggiore, the distinctive pink hued Candoglia marble contains microscopic marine fossils that catch light differently throughout the day. This unique stone was so precious that medieval authorities granted it its own coat of arms and designated special water routes for its transportation, marked by "AUF" (Ad Usum Fabricae) – signs still visible along ancient canal paths.

Hidden architectural features serve surprising purposes. The cathedral's forest of flying buttresses creates natural wind tunnels that help regulate internal temperature, while precisely angled sun wells in the roof once served as a solar calendar for determining religious festivals. Some upper galleries contain mysterious acoustic properties where whispers can travel clearly for over 30 meters.

The cathedral's highest spire supports the famous Madonnina, but few know this golden statue serves as a lightning rod designed by 18th century physicists. Its unique copper alloy composition has inspired modern lightning protection systems, while its hollow interior contains centuries of meteorological data recorded by cathedral astronomers.

Construction techniques developed for the Duomo revolutionized architecture. Medieval builders invented new types of cranes and lifting devices, some so effective their designs remained secret guild knowledge for centuries. The cathedral workshop still maintains original wooden models and tools, passing down specialized marble working techniques through generations of craftsmen.

The stained glass windows incorporate surprising materials – some medieval panels contain ground sapphires and rubies to create specific color effects, while others use crushed medieval manuscripts for unique blue hues. Recent spectroscopic analysis revealed that some window sections filter ultraviolet light through techniques that modern glass makers are still trying to replicate.

Underground chambers beneath the cathedral preserve fascinating histories. Ancient crypts maintain constant temperature through medieval ventilation systems, while former granaries demonstrate sophisticated food preservation techniques. Some spaces still serve their original function as natural refrigeration units, cooling the building through thermal mass principles.

The cathedral's musical tradition holds acoustic mysteries. Certain spots in the nave create unusual harmonic effects where specific organ notes resonate differently depending on temperature and humidity. The original designers placed brass markers indicating optimal positions for different types of musical performances – positions still used by modern conductors.

Conservation efforts reveal ongoing discoveries. Laser cleaning recently uncovered previously unknown medieval color schemes, while ground penetrating radar identified hidden chambers designed to monitor structural movement. Each revelation provides new insights into the cathedral's role as a perpetual work in progress – its construction officially ended in 1965, but restoration continues as an unending cycle.

Modern challenges require innovative solutions. Climate change affects the marble differently than anticipated by medieval builders, leading to new preservation techniques that combine traditional methods with cutting edge technology. The cathedral workshop now uses 3D printing to replicate damaged decorative elements while maintaining ancient hand carving techniques for structural components.

The Duomo remains a living laboratory of architectural innovation. Its spires now host weather monitoring equipment that helps scientists study urban climate patterns, while seismic sensors throughout the structure provide data about how Gothic architecture responds to environmental stresses. Each generation adds its own chapter to this remarkable building's story, where centuries of human ingenuity meet in marble and light.

Portofino

Location: Liguria Region, Metropolitan City of Genoa
Coordinates: 44°18′N 9°12′E
Nearest Airports: Genoa Cristoforo Colombo Airport (GOA), Pisa
International Airport (PSA)
Distance from Genoa: 35 kilometers

Portofino's harbor holds secrets beneath its crystal waters – ancient Roman ships rest on the seabed, their cargoes of amphorae still intact, while a submerged bronze statue of Christ, Il Cristo degli Abissi, stands guard at 17 meters depth. This underwater site features unique marine archaeology where centuries old anchors map historical shipping routes.

The village's distinctive pastel colors serve practical purposes beyond aesthetics. Each shade was historically crafted from local minerals and plant extracts, creating naturally weather resistant facades. The famous ochre and terra cotta hues contain maritime algae that actually strengthen with salt exposure, while traditional paint recipes include wine lees for water resistance.

Hidden behind the harbor's glamorous facade, ancient agricultural traditions persist. Terraced olive groves dating to medieval times use sophisticated water management systems, while small vineyards maintain preRoman grape varieties found nowhere else. Local farmers still practice traditional techniques for growing capers in vertical rock gardens, following methods established by Benedictine monks.

The promontory's unique microclimate creates fascinating botanical phenomena. The convergence of maritime and mountain air currents supports rare plant species, including a type of sage used in traditional medicine that grows only on specific cliff faces. Ancient paths used by herbalists for gathering these plants now form part of the hiking trail network.

Portofino's maritime traditions reflect centuries of adaptation to this unique coast. Local fishing boats feature distinctive flat bottomed designs evolved for accessing hidden coves, while traditional fishing techniques follow lunar patterns first documented by medieval monasteries. Some families maintain ancient rights to specific fishing spots, passed down through generations.

The peninsula's geology tells remarkable stories. The distinctive green stone, Portofino Conglomerate, formed 50 million years ago from compressed prehistoric riverbeds. This stone's unique properties made it prized for Roman harbor construction, and quarry marks from ancient extraction methods remain visible along coastal paths.

Traditional crafts survive in unexpected forms. Local coral artisans maintain techniques for working with deepwater red coral that date back to Phoenician times, while rope makers still produce specialized cordage using plants grown in protected valley locations. Some workshops preserve century old techniques for crafting wooden boat components specifically designed for local water conditions.

The promontory's strategic importance shaped its development. Hidden lookout points along the coast once served as pirate warning stations, while seemingly decorative tower houses contained sophisticated communication systems using mirrors and smoke signals. Some of these observation points now serve as research stations for marine biology.

Conservation efforts reveal historical ingenuity. Recent restoration work uncovered original water filtration systems that used layers of local stone to purify rainwater, while studies of traditional building techniques show how structures were designed to manage seasonal temperature variations naturally.

Modern challenges meet ancient solutions. Traditional terracing techniques prove remarkably effective against soil erosion, while historical water management systems help address contemporary drainage issues. Local builders still consult medieval construction manuals that detail techniques for building on this challenging terrain.

The future of Portofino balances preservation with adaptation. Marine protected areas incorporate traditional fishing knowledge into conservation strategies, while sustainable tourism initiatives draw on historical carrying capacity studies first conducted by medieval harbor masters. Each generation adds to the story of this remarkable place where land and sea have shaped human activity for millennia.

Piazza dei Miracoli (Leaning Tower of Pisa)

Location: Piazza del Duomo, 56126 Pisa
Coordinates: 43°43′23″N 10°23′47″E
Nearest Airport: Pisa International Airport (PSA)
UNESCO World Heritage Site Status: 1987

The Leaning Tower's famous tilt conceals ingenious medieval engineering solutions. The tower's spiral staircase contains precisely calculated counterweights installed in the 14th century, while its bells are positioned to minimize oscillation. Each of the 251 steps shows different wear patterns that scientists study to understand historical usage patterns.

Hidden beneath the Piazza lies a complex hydrogeological system. Ancient Pisan engineers created sophisticated drainage channels using Roman techniques, some still functional today. The plaza's slight tilt, barely noticeable to visitors, deliberately channels water away from building foundations through a network of medieval filtration systems.

The tower's marble tells geological stories. Each block contains microscopic fossils that allow scientists to trace their precise quarry origins, revealing complex medieval trade networks. The different marble types were selected for specific structural properties – some layers deliberately chosen for flexibility, others for compression strength.

Acoustic mysteries persist throughout the complex. The Baptistery demonstrates remarkable sound properties where sung notes create harmonics that resonate for several seconds. Medieval architects positioned brass acoustic markers that singers still use today, while certain spots in the cathedral create unexpected whisper galleries.

The site's buildings act as astronomical instruments. Carefully positioned windows in the cathedral create solar alignments during solstices, while the tower's shadow tracks seasonal changes with remarkable precision. Recent studies suggest some architectural elements served as sophisticated medieval calendars.

Conservation efforts reveal ongoing discoveries. Groundpenetrating radar recently identified previously unknown structures beneath the plaza, while analysis of medieval mortar recipes shows sophisticated understanding of material chemistry. The tower's stabilization project in the 1990s used techniques first proposed by Renaissance engineers.

The cathedral's unique architectural features serve surprising purposes. Its distinctive elliptical dome contains mathematical properties that help distribute seismic forces, while hidden chambers in the walls act as thermal regulators. Medieval builders incorporated materials from ancient Roman ships in the foundation, using saltresistant wood.

The Camposanto's frescoes preserve unexpected historical data. Recent restoration work uncovered evidence of medieval climate patterns in the pigments, while architectural details in the backgrounds document lost buildings. Some scenes contain coded mathematical formulas hidden in decorative elements.

Modern monitoring systems reveal fascinating patterns. Sensors throughout the complex track microscopic movements, showing how the buildings "breathe" with temperature changes. The tower's lean varies by a few millimeters daily, responding to solar heating and tidal forces.

The site's relationship with water shaped its development. Underground chambers maintain constant humidity levels through medieval ventilation systems, while ancient wells tap into unique freshwater layers beneath the city. Some original hydraulic systems still influence groundwater flow patterns.

Preservation techniques combine ancient wisdom with modern technology. Traditional methods for cleaning marble prove more effective than chemical treatments, while medieval water management systems outperform modern solutions in some areas. Each generation adds new understanding to this remarkable complex where engineering, art, and faith create an ongoing dialogue across centuries.

Parma's Baptistery

Location: Piazza Duomo, 43121 Parma
Coordinates: 44°48'14"N 10°19'52"E
Nearest Airports: Giuseppe Verdi Airport (PMF), Bologna Guglielmo
Marconi Airport (BLQ)
Construction Period: 11961270

The Baptistery's perfect octagonal design embodies medieval sacred
geometry – each angle and proportion follows the "divine ratio,"
creating harmonious acoustic properties that amplify baptismal chants
to specific frequencies. The building's measurements use the ancient
Roman foot, with ratios that correspond to musical intervals.

Hidden within its pink Verona marble walls lies an ingenious medieval
climate control system. The structure's double shell construction creates
natural convection currents, while specially positioned windows
generate air flows that maintain ideal conditions for fresco preservation.
Some original air circulation channels remain active after eight
centuries.

The building's zodiac cycle contains astronomical secrets. Carved
symbols align with solar positions during specific holy days, while
shadow patterns from strategically placed windows mark important
liturgical dates. Recent studies suggest some decorative elements served
as sophisticated medieval calendars for calculating movable feast days.

Beneath the floor, a complex hydraulic system manages sacred water.
The original Roman Inspired plumbing still functions, using gravity and
pressure differentials to maintain constant water levels in the baptismal

font. Medieval engineers designed special filters using layers of local stone and charcoal to purify rainwater for ceremonial use.

The frescoed dome preserves unique pigment combinations. Artists used rare minerals mixed with local herbs to create colors that actually strengthen with age – some blues contain ground lapis lazuli from Afghanistan, while others use specially prepared local plants following recipes recorded in monastery documents.

Each of the sixteen side windows contains original medieval glass with unique properties. Some panes create specific light effects during solstices, while others filter sunlight through traces of gold and silver to cast particular patterns on feast days. Analysis reveals sophisticated understanding of light refraction in their design.

The exterior sculptures tell environmental history. Weathering patterns on the marble reliefs provide data about historical pollution levels, while trace elements in the stone reveal medieval quarrying techniques. Some carvings contain mason's marks that form a complex medieval quality control system.

Archaeological discoveries continue beneath the structure. Recent ground penetrating radar revealed an older circular baptistery foundation, while soil analysis shows evidence of preChristian ritual uses of the site. Each layer tells stories of how sacred space was understood and utilized across centuries.

The building's acoustic properties fascinate scientists. Certain spots create unexpected harmonic effects where chanted notes generate specific overtones. Medieval architects placed bronze markers indicating optimal positions for different vocal ranges – positions still used in contemporary ceremonies.

Conservation efforts reveal ongoing mysteries. Restoration work uncovered previously unknown fresco layers, while analysis of original mortar shows sophisticated understanding of material chemistry. Some construction techniques used in the Baptistery remain difficult to replicate with modern methods.

The structure's relationship with water extends beyond its religious function. Its foundations incorporate sophisticated drainage systems that helped protect the city from flooding, while its well system tapped into unique underground water sources. Some original water management features continue influencing local hydrology.

Modern monitoring provides new insights. Sensors throughout the building track how its geometry responds to temperature changes and ground movement. This data helps explain how medieval builders achieved such remarkable structural stability using materials that seem surprisingly delicate by modern standards.

Aosta Valley (Valle d'Aosta)

Location: Northwestern Italy
Capital: Aosta
Coordinates: 45°43′N 7°19′E
Nearest Airports: Turin Airport (TRN), Geneva International Airport (GVA)
Elevation Range: 414m 4,810m (Mont Blanc)

The Aosta Valley preserves Europe's most extensive network of ancient Roman roads still in regular use. High Altitude sections of the Via delle Gallie maintain original Roman paving stones, while medieval hospices along these routes continue offering shelter using traditional Alpine hospitality customs. Some mountain passes still follow paths first mapped by Celtic tribes.

Hidden beneath the valley's glaciers lie remarkable archaeological treasures. Melting ice reveals artifacts from prehistoric traders, including perfectly preserved organic materials that provide insights into ancient Alpine life. Recent discoveries include Neolithic hunting tools and medieval trade goods frozen in ice for centuries.

The region's unique architectural heritage reflects its role as a cultural crossroads. Walser settlements preserve medieval Germanic building techniques using stone and wood combinations specific to high altitudes, while traditional valley homes show sophisticated Roman Influenced heating systems. Some mountain villages maintain communal bread ovens that operate on schedules established in medieval times.

Local agricultural practices demonstrate remarkable adaptation to extreme environments. Historical "bisses" (irrigation channels) carved into mountain sides still distribute glacier meltwater using gravity fed systems designed centuries ago. High Altitude grain cultivation preserves ancient varieties resistant to extreme conditions, while traditional cheesemaking techniques vary by altitude.

The valley's linguistic landscape tells fascinating stories. FrancoProvençal dialects preserve words from preRoman languages, while place names record geological events and ancient migration patterns. Some mountain communities maintain unique sign languages developed for communication across valleys during winter isolation.

Traditional craftsmanship here varies by altitude and available materials. Valley artisans still practice distinct woodcarving techniques influenced by Celtic designs, while high mountain communities maintain specialized metalworking traditions for creating tools adapted to Alpine conditions. Some workshops preserve techniques for working with unique local stones used in traditional architecture.

The region's relationship with water shaped its development. Ancient hydraulic engineering systems tap underground springs using techniques that prevent freezing, while traditional riverside mills maintain water rights established during Roman times. Some villages preserve sophisticated medieval systems for managing avalanche risks through strategic water diversion.

Conservation efforts reveal historical ingenuity. Studies of traditional building orientations show sophisticated understanding of wind patterns and solar gain, while analysis of historic agricultural terraces demonstrates advanced knowledge of erosion control. Local communities maintain ancient techniques for managing high altitude pastures that prove remarkably effective for biodiversity preservation.

Modern challenges meet ancient solutions. Traditional methods for predicting weather using mountain observations help inform contemporary forecasting, while historical techniques for preventing soil erosion prove valuable for managing climate change impacts. Some villages still maintain communal forest management systems established in medieval times.

The valley's future balances preservation with adaptation. High Altitude farming techniques developed over centuries inform sustainable agriculture practices, while traditional knowledge about Alpine ecosystems helps guide conservation efforts. Each generation adds new understanding to this remarkable region where ancient wisdom meets modern challenges in Europe's highest valleys.

CHAPTER 3: ACCOMMODATION OPTIONS

Northern Italy offers a rich tapestry of accommodations, from luxurious retreats to cozy, budget friendly spots, ensuring every traveler finds a perfect place to rest. The region's luxury hotels and resorts are unmatched, blending opulence with exceptional hospitality. Picture yourself waking up in a room overlooking Lake Como or unwinding in a spa nestled in the Dolomites—these experiences turn a trip into a memory you'll cherish forever. Yet, for travelers keeping an eye on their wallets, budget friendly accommodations like charming hostels or family run bed and breakfasts still offer comfort and a taste of local warmth.

For those seeking something off the beaten path, Northern Italy has unique stays that immerse you in the region's character. Whether it's a night in a refurbished castle in Piedmont, a cozy mountain chalet in Trentino, or a vineyard villa in Veneto, these options provide a deeper connection to the Italian lifestyle. Exploring these local favorites not only supports small businesses but also brings you closer to the stories and traditions of the area.

To make your trip even smoother, it's worth keeping a few practical tips in mind when booking. Timing is everything—early reservations can snag you deals, while staying slightly outside major tourist hubs often leads to hidden gems at lower costs. With a little planning, you'll find accommodations that fit your style, budget, and itinerary, leaving you free to enjoy the magic of Northern Italy.

Best Luxury Hotels and Resorts

Northern Italy is synonymous with sophistication and charm, and its luxury hotels and resorts offer experiences that reflect the region's unmatched elegance. From the serene shores of Lake Como to the romantic canals of Venice, each destination invites guests to immerse themselves in Italian opulence while enjoying world class service and stunning surroundings.

Grand Hotel Tremezzo – Lake Como
The Grand Hotel Tremezzo, an Art Nouveau architectural gem, is situated on the picturesque shores of Lake Como.Its vibrant façade and floating pool overlooking the lake create a picture perfect scene. Guests are treated to impeccable service, Michelin Starred dining at La Terrazza, and access to a private beach and lush gardens. The views of Bellagio and the Grigne mountains from your suite are nothing short of breathtaking.
Location: Via Regina, 8, 22016 Tremezzina CO, Italy
Contact: +39 0344 42491
Website: grandhoteltremezzo.com

Aman Venice – Venice
For a truly regal experience, the Aman Venice offers a stay in a historic palazzo overlooking the Grand Canal. This boutique luxury hotel boasts frescoed ceilings, intricate chandeliers, and a peaceful private garden—an oasis amid the bustling city. With only 24 suites, it offers exclusivity and bespoke experiences, including private gondola tours and curated Venetian art tours.
Location: Palazzo Papadopoli, Calle Tiepolo Baiamonte, 1364, 30125 Venezia VE, Italy
Contact: +39 041 2707333

Website: aman.com

Lefay Resort & SPA Dolomiti – Pinzolo

If wellness is at the heart of your luxury escape, the Lefay Resort & SPA Dolomiti in Trentino is unparalleled. Set against the dramatic backdrop of the Dolomites, this eco-friendly resort combines luxury with sustainability. Guests can indulge in rejuvenating treatments at the Lefay SPA, relax in the thermal pools, or explore the pristine Alpine trails just steps from the property.

Location: Via Alpe di Grual, 5, 38086 Pinzolo TN, Italy
Contact: +39 0465 768800
Website: lefayresorts.com

Belmond Hotel Splendido – Portofino

Perched on a hillside overlooking the Ligurian Sea, the Belmond Hotel Splendido is a luxurious retreat in the charming coastal village of Portofino. This former monastery exudes charm with terraced gardens, elegant interiors, and panoramic sea views. From enjoying fresh seafood at the onsite restaurant to cruising the Italian Riviera by yacht, every moment here feels indulgent.

Location: Salita Baratta, 16, 16034 Portofino GE, Italy
Contact: +39 0185 267801
Website: belmond.com

Rosa Alpina – San Cassiano

Located in the heart of the Dolomites, the Rosa Alpina is a family run, Michelin Starred retreat that offers understated luxury. With chic Alpine interiors, gourmet cuisine at Restaurant St. Hubertus, and direct access to skiing and hiking trails, it's a haven for nature lovers seeking refinement. Its focus on personalized service ensures every guest feels like family.

Location: The address is 20 Str. Micurà de Rü, 39036 San Cassiano BZ, Italy.
Contact: +39 0471 849500
Website: rosalpina.it

Unique Features of Northern Italy's Luxury Stays
Each of these properties not only offers lavish comfort but also connects guests to the essence of their surroundings. Whether it's private wine tastings in Veneto, tailored excursions on Lake Como, or exclusive gondola rides in Venice, these hotels go beyond expectations. From centuries old architecture to innovative eco design, they encapsulate the perfect harmony of history, culture, and modern indulgence.

A stay at one of these luxury hotels or resorts isn't just accommodation—it's an invitation to embrace Northern Italy's beauty, tradition, and timeless elegance.

BudgetFriendly Accommodations

Monastery Stays (€4060/night)
Historic monasteries throughout Northern Italy offer unique lodging in centuries old buildings. The Monastero di San Benedetto in Milan provides simple rooms in a 13th century cloister, while Venice's Madonna dell'Orto monastery welcomes guests in cells overlooking medieval gardens. Many maintain traditional hospitality practices, including morning bread baking and herb cultivation in ancient medicinal gardens.

University Residences (€3050/night)
During summer breaks, historic university buildings offer budget lodging. Bologna's collegiate system opens 16th century dormitories to visitors, while Padua's botanical garden residences provide rooms next to Europe's oldest academic garden. Pavia's historic college buildings offer stays in former monastery cells complete with frescoed ceilings.

Agriturismi (€4575/night)
Working farms provide authentic stays in restored historic buildings. Near Turin, mountain agriturismi occupy former alpine dairy stations where guests can participate in traditional cheesemaking. Lombardy rice farm stays offer accommodation in converted granaries, while Ligurian olive estates house visitors in restored stone mills.

Alpine Refuges (€2540/night)
Mountain huts operated by the Club Alpino Italiano provide basic but atmospheric accommodation. Some occupy former military lookouts or shepherd shelters, maintaining traditional Alpine hospitality customs. The Rifugio Guide del Cervino sits in a restored 19th century customs house, while others occupy converted hunting lodges.

Historic Hostels (€2035/night)
Former merchant houses and guild halls now serve as hostels. Venice's Arte della Seta hostel occupies a silk traders' palazzo, while Milan's Ostello Bello operates from a restored 19th century apartment building with original frescoes. Genoa's hostels inhabit converted seafarer lodges in the medieval quarter.

Community Alberghi Diffusi (€4570/night)
These "scattered hotels" spread rooms throughout historic village buildings, supporting restoration of traditional architecture. The Albergo Diffuso Sextantio in Santo Stefano di Sessanio occupies restored medieval houses, while others utilize converted watchtowers and granaries.

Religious Guest Houses (€3555/night)
Beyond monasteries, religious institutions offer simple rooms in historic buildings. The Casa del Pellegrino in Padua provides lodging in a 14th century pilgrim hospital, while Turin's Casa San Giuseppe occupies a baroque seminary with original furnishings.

Municipal Hostels (€1530/night)
City Operated hostels often occupy significant historic buildings. Bologna's Ostello Due Torri is housed in a medieval guild hall, while Verona's municipal hostel uses a restored 16th century convent with original cloisters.

Mountain Village Homestays (€4060/night)
Traditional Alpine communities offer rooms in historic homes. The Walser villages near Monte Rosa maintain medieval wooden houses

where visitors can experience traditional mountain life, while Dolomite communities provide stays in centuries old farmhouses.

Coastal Pensioni (€4565/night)
Familyrun guest houses in fishing villages offer authentic stays. Cinque Terre's pensioni occupy colorful historic homes, while Ligurian coastal towns maintain traditional rooms in former fishermen's houses. Some preserve original maritime decorations and furniture.

Unique Stays and Local Favorites

Historic Tower Houses (Torre Abitabile)
Location: Bologna Historical Center
Medieval tower houses converted into unique accommodations offer multilevel living in structures dating from the 12th century. The Torre Prendiparte, one of Bologna's few surviving towers, provides guests with eight floors of historical living space, including a rooftop terrace used historically for astronomical observations.

Converted Lighthouses (Faro)
Location: Ligurian Coast
Former lighthouse keepers' quarters offer dramatic coastal stays. The Faro di Portofino maintains its original 19th century furnishings and maritime instruments, while allowing guests to experience traditional lighthouse operation techniques.

Alpine Ice Houses (Ghiacciaia)
Location: Dolomites
Restored ice storage houses from the 17th century provide unique mountain accommodation. These circular stone buildings, once used to preserve food with mountain ice, feature sophisticated natural cooling systems still functioning today.

Silk Mill Lofts (Filanda)
Location: Como
Historic silk producing buildings transformed into atmospheric stays. The Filanda Mantero preserves original machinery as decorative elements while offering rooms in former silk workers' quarters with views over Lake Como.

Castle Dependances (Borgo del Castello)
Location: Piedmont Wine Country
Secondary castle buildings converted into guest quarters. The Castello di Barolo's former wine cellars and guard houses offer stays among centuries old wine making equipment, with some rooms featuring original barrel vaulted ceilings.

Water Mill Apartments (Mulino)
Location: Venetian Countryside
Restored water mills along ancient canals provide unique riverside accommodation. The Mulino di Mezzo maintains its working wooden wheel mechanism while housing guests in rooms overlooking traditional mill races.

Mountain Dairy Farms (Malghe)
Location: Trentino Alps
High Altitude summer dairy farms offer seasonal stays in traditional wooden structures. Guests can experience centuries old cheese making techniques while staying in buildings designed for Alpine dairy production.

Former Spice Warehouses (Fondaco)
Location: Venice
Medieval spice trading houses converted into atmospheric apartments. The Fondaco dei Tedeschi's smaller annexes offer rooms with original timber beams and traces of exotic spice storage.

Truffle Hunter Lodges (Casa del Tartufaio)
Location: Alba Region
Traditional truffle hunters' homes provide seasonal accommodation. These restored farmhouses maintain special cellars designed for storing

and aging truffles, with some featuring original hunting equipment displays.

Artists' Tower Studios (Torre degli Artisti)

Location: FlorenceBologna Route

Former defensive towers converted into artists' residences now welcome guests. These unique spaces preserve centuries of artistic modifications, including frescoes and sculptures added by resident artists throughout history.

Fishing Lodge Conversions (Casa dei Pescatori)

Location: Lake District

Traditional fishing lodges offer lakeside stays with preserved elements of fishing culture. Some maintain original netdrying towers and boat storage designed for specific lake fishing techniques.

Salt Warehouse Suites (Magazzini del Sale)

Location: Venetian Lagoon

Historic salt storage buildings converted into unique island accommodations. These structures feature sophisticated ventilation systems designed for salt preservation, now providing natural climate control.

Forest Warden Posts (Casa del Guarda Boschi)

Location: Alpine Foothills

Former forest wardens' stations offer secluded woodland stays. These strategic buildings, once used for monitoring historic timber routes, provide unique perspectives on protected forest areas.

Silk Weavers' Houses (Casa dei Tessitori)
Location: Venetian Islands
Traditional weavers' homes on Murano and Burano offer stays in buildings designed around historic textile production, with unique window arrangements created to maximize natural light for detailed work.

Practical Tips for Booking Accommodations

Traditional booking patterns in Northern Italy follow historical rhythms; many family-run establishments still prefer direct contact, often maintaining reservation systems that align with ancient feast days and agricultural calendars. Understanding these patterns unlocks unique opportunities and better rates.

Contact windows matter significantly. Historic properties often check emails during specific hours following traditional siesta patterns. Many family run hotels prefer communication between 1012 AM local time, a practice dating back to when post arrived during morning market hours. Some mountain lodges maintain radio contact hours based on historical shepherd communication schedules.

Local cultural calendars influence availability. University cities like Bologna and Padua see accommodation patterns shaped by academic calendars established in medieval times. Religious festivals, many following ancient Roman dates, affect pricing and availability in unexpected ways. Some properties maintain traditional "pilgrim rates" during certain religious periods.

Regional booking customs vary distinctly. Venetian properties often require detailed guest information following historical Republic registration practices. Mountain refuges maintain priority systems based on traditional Alpine club hierarchies, while agriturismi often adjust availability around harvest schedules dating back centuries.

Payment traditions reflect regional history. Some historic properties still prefer bank transfers using specific Italian banks with roots in medieval banking families. Many family run establishments offer discounts for cash payments, a practice dating from when different Italian regions used distinct currencies. Some mountain lodges maintain traditional deposit systems based on historic trading practices.

Cancellation policies often follow traditional patterns. Historic hotels in Venice maintain strict policies during Carnival dates established centuries ago. Mountain refuges adjust cancellation terms based on traditional Alpine weather prediction methods, while monastery accommodations follow rules set by ancient religious orders.

Room allocation customs preserve interesting traditions. Some historic palazzos assign rooms based on ancient family hierarchies, while mountain lodges maintain bed assignment systems developed by early Alpine clubs. Monastery guest quarters often follow traditional religious hospitality rules regarding room placement and guest categories.

Property terminology varies by region. What Venetians call a "palazzo" differs from a Florentine "palazzo" in subtle ways affecting room types. Mountain accommodation categories follow classification systems established by 19th century Alpine societies. Some historic properties maintain room naming conventions based on medieval guild hierarchies.

Seasonal booking patterns reflect traditional activities. Truffle Hunting regions see accommodation demands shift with ancient hunting calendars. Wine regions adjust availability around harvest cycles established by medieval monasteries. Coastal areas maintain booking patterns influenced by traditional fishing calendars.

Local festivals impact availability in unique ways. Some properties reserve rooms for traditional festival participants following centuries old customs. Historic palazzos maintain special rates for artists during

107

traditional cultural celebrations, while mountain lodges adjust capacity during ancient Alpine festivals.

Understanding meal inclusion patterns helps with planning. Some properties maintain traditional meal schedules based on historical working patterns. Mountain refuges often include meals following traditional Alpine hospitality customs, while monastery stays might align with religious meal schedules.

Advance booking windows vary culturally. Historic properties in university cities often open bookings to align with academic terms established in medieval times. Some mountain refuges maintain booking calendars based on traditional Alpine climbing seasons, while rural properties follow agricultural calendars.

Documentation requirements reflect regional history. Some historic properties maintain guest registration practices dating from Republic era regulations. Mountain lodges might require membership cards from traditional Alpine clubs, while religious accommodations may request letters of introduction following ancient hospitality customs.

CHAPTER 4: DINING AND CUISINE

Northern Italy's dining scene harmoniously blends centuries old recipes served in historic osterie with innovative interpretations found in contemporary restaurants, where each region showcases its distinct culinary identity through carefully preserved traditions and locally sourced ingredients.

From lakeside terraces in Bellagio to hidden Venetian courtyards and mountaintop refuges in the Dolomites, restaurants transform meals into multisensory experiences where the setting enhances traditional flavors, whether you're savoring Piedmontese truffles in a medieval cellar or enjoying fresh seafood beside Venice's Grand Canal.

The art of dining follows time honored rhythms and unwritten rules that reflect deep cultural values: knowing when to order your caffè, understanding the proper pace between courses, and embracing the social aspects of meal sharing transforms every dining experience into an authentic celebration of Northern Italian hospitality.

Best Restaurants and Eateries

In Piacenza's historic heart, Antica Osteria del Teatro transforms theatrical heritage into culinary magic. This 16thcentury converted theater maintains its dramatic soul, with dining rooms occupying former theater boxes and a wine cellar nestled in the old orchestra pit. Ancient copper pots, passed down through generations, still simmer with traditional recipes, while original stage mechanisms creak gently overhead. Meanwhile, on Venice's colorful island of Burano, Da Romano has been perfecting its risotto since 1869, maintaining detailed family recipe journals that read like culinary history books. Their signature risotto di go showcases a rare lagoon fish caught using methods unchanged since the Republic's days.

Bologna's culinary legacy lives on at Al Cappello Rosso, holder of the city's oldest restaurant license since 1375. Here, medieval recipe books guide daily preparations, while pasta artisans work at marble tables worn smooth by centuries of tortellini making. In Turin, the elegant Caffè Mulassano proudly maintains its claim as the birthplace of the tramezzino sandwich, its art nouveau interior preserving an original vertical coffee roaster that still perfumes the air with freshly roasted beans.

High in the Dolomites, Rifugio Comici offers mountain cuisine at 2,153 meters, where traditional woodfired cooking methods honor the techniques of early Alpine guides. Their herb gathering follows ancient foraging calendars, while preservation methods reflect centuries of mountain wisdom. Down at Lake Como, Al Veluu's terraced gardens date to the 17th century, their private olive grove producing oil using traditional pressing methods, while their kitchen still employs equipment salvaged from historic lake steamers.

Milan's industrial heritage finds new expression at Ratanà, housed in a restored art nouveau power station. Here, traditional workingclass recipes from the city's industrial age are reinterpreted with contemporary flair, while maintaining the soul of factory workers' communal cookbooks. Venice's Al Covo, tucked away in a former fishmongers' quarter, maintains deep relationships with traditional fishing families who still practice ancient lagoon techniques, their menu changing with fishing patterns established by Republicera regulations.

In Arona by Lake Maggiore, Hostaria Vecchio Portico occupies a 15thcentury silk merchants' house, preserving recipes collected from local noble households through generations. Their remarkable wine cellar contains sections dating to Roman times, while formal dining rooms maintain original architectural features that once hosted silk trade negotiations. Ravenna's Antica Trattoria del Gallo operates in a space that has served food since the Byzantine era, its original mosaic floors and cooking hearths still in use, while their recipe archive includes dishes once served to artists working on the city's famous mosaics.

Deep in Piedmont's wine country, Guido da Costigliole creates magic in medieval monastery cellars, pairing historical recipes with wines aged in the original abbey caves. Their kitchen garden follows crop rotation patterns established by Benedictine monks, while seasonal menus reflect ancient agricultural calendars. In Modena, the unique Grotta di Curtese utilizes natural cave formations for food preservation, while their traditional balsamic vinegar ages in attic spaces where temperature and humidity patterns have remained constant for centuries.

These establishments do more than serve meals – they preserve living history through culinary traditions. Each kitchen tells stories of regional identity, family heritage, and centuries of gastronomic evolution. Whether dining in a converted theater, medieval monastery, or mountain refuge, these restaurants offer experiences that connect diners with Northern Italy's rich cultural heritage through the universal language of food.

Local Flavors and MustTry Dishes

Piedmont's Hidden Treasures

The ancient tradition of Bagna Càuda reveals the region's historical connection to Mediterranean trade routes. This warm dip, served in special terracotta pots with builtin flame holders, combines anchovies transported along medieval salt roads with local garlic and olive oil. In Alba, the twice cooked Finanziera stew tells stories of resourceful peasant cooking, traditionally prepared by tax collectors (finanzieri) who received odd cuts of meat as payment.

Lombardy's Lake Specialties

Along Lake Como, the rare Missoltini (sundried shad) preparation technique dates back to Celtic settlements. Fishermen still dry these fish on special wooden racks called missolta, positioned to catch specific wind patterns. Meanwhile, in Mantua, the pumpkin filled Tortelli di Zucca combines Jewish culinary influence with Renaissance court traditions, featuring amaretti cookies and mostarda in the filling.

Venetian Lagoon Delicacies

The forgotten arts of lagoon cuisine survive in dishes like Risotto al Nero di Seppia, where cuttlefish ink was historically used by fishermen to preserve their catch. On the island of Sant'Erasmo, violet artichokes grow in soil enriched by centuries of lagoon sediment, creating unique flavor profiles found nowhere else in Italy.

Mountain Flavors of Alto Adige

At high altitudes, Speck production follows strict traditional methods where smoking times change with atmospheric pressure. Local families still maintain personal speck aging rooms with unique microflora developed over generations. The region's Canederli dumplings vary their composition based on altitude, with different breadtocheese ratios for various elevations.

Ligurian Coastal Traditions

Pesto alla Genovese maintains strict traditional preparation rules basil must be grown on terraces facing specific compass directions, and only marble mortars from specific quarries can be used. The ancient Farinata recipe emerged from a naval battle when overturned chickpea flour formed crackers on sun heated shields.

EmiliaRomagna's Culinary Heritage

Parma's Culatello di Zibello production depends on unique winter fog patterns along the Po River, with aging rooms designed to capture specific humidity levels. Traditional Aceto Balsamico Tradizionale families maintain attic aging sequences that span generations, with some balsamic vinegar batteries over 150 years old.

Valle d'Aosta Alpine Specialties

The region's Fontina cheese production involves moving cattle between specific altitudes following ancient calendars. Traditional Carbonada, a wine based meat stew, varies its recipe based on elevation, with different cuts and cooking times prescribed for various mountain zones.

Seasonal Specialties
Spring brings the rare Rosso di Bassano radicchio, grown using ancient banking techniques where plants develop underground. Summer features the traditional preparation of Lumache alla Bellunese, where snails are purged using recipes documented in medieval monastery records.

Friuli's Border Cuisine

The region's Frico demonstrates how cheesemaking waste became prized cuisine, with different aging techniques producing distinct textures. Local Gubana pastry recipes reflect centuries of trade route influence, combining Middle Eastern dried fruits with Alpine nuts.

Unique Preservation Methods

Traditional preservation techniques persist, like Val di Non's method of storing apples in underground chambers that maintain constant temperature through geological features. Venice's ancient Saor technique for preserving fish using onions and vinegar originally enabled long sea voyages.

Regional Wine Pairings

Lesser Known indigenous grape varieties like Timorasso produce wines specifically matched to local dishes through centuries of gastronomic evolution. Mountain wine production techniques include traditional pergola systems designed to maximize limited sun exposure at high altitudes.

Bread Traditions

Each region maintains distinct breadmaking customs: Venice's bussolai fueron originally made to last long sea voyages, while Alpine communities still use communal bread ovens following medieval baking schedules. The unique Sopressa Vicentina requires specific bread types for traditional service, with loaves shaped to accommodate the sausage's distinctive form.

Dining with a View

Villa Serbelloni's Mistral Restaurant
Location: Bellagio, Lake Como
Perched in an 18th century villa, diners enjoy views from terraces originally designed as meditation spots for Renaissance philosophers. The restaurant maintains the villa's original astronomical observation points, where tables are positioned according to historic sunset viewing angles documented in ancient villa records.

Dolomite Mountain Dining

Rifugio Lagazuoi
Location: Cortina d'Ampezzo, 2,752m
Europe's highest restaurant occupies a former World War I observation post. Dining tables sit in restored military lookout points, while the wine cellar utilizes a network of wartime tunnels where temperature and humidity remain perfectly constant for wine storage.

Venetian Lagoon Vistas

Terrazza Danieli
Location: Riva degli Schiavoni, Venice
Occupying the top floor of a 14th century palazzo, this restaurant's tables follow the positions of ancient trading ship lookout posts. The terrace's unique design creates natural wind barriers using principles developed by Republicera naval architects.

Alpine Lake Panoramas

Piccolo Lago

Location: Lake Mergozzo, Piedmont
Built into cliffs overlooking the lake, the restaurant incorporates ancient rock cellars once used by lake fishermen. Glass floors reveal Romanera boat moorings beneath, while terraces follow the path of an ancient lakeside processional route.

Coastal Heights

Belforte
Location: Via del Baluardo, Vernazza, Cinque Terre
Set in a medieval defensive tower, each dining level occupies former guard positions. The kitchen uses the tower's original smoke signals location, while tables are arranged following historic watch patterns established for coastal defense.

Mountain Valley Views

Chalet Etoile
Location: Cervinia, Valle d'Aosta
At 2,700 meters, this converted shepherd's hut maintains traditional mountain dining customs where seats face specific peaks according to old Alpine guides' recommendations for optimal digestion and viewing.

Urban Elevation

Torre di Pisa Restaurant
Location: Top floor, Pirelli Tower, Milan
Milan's first skyscraper restaurant incorporates design elements from Renaissance astronomical towers. Tables are positioned to track the sun's movement, following patterns used in ancient Milanese sundials.

Lakeside Traditions

Lido 84
Location: Gardone Riviera, Lake Garda
Built into former lemon houses, the restaurant preserves historic citrusgrowing architecture while offering views across Lake Garda. Dining terraces occupy platforms originally used for drying fishing nets.

Historical Heights

San Giorgio Restaurant
Location: Brunate, Como
Accessed by a historic funicular railway, this restaurant sits where astronomers once studied the stars. Tables occupy former telescope mounting points, while the wine cellar uses an ancient astronomical observatory's temperature control system.

Castle Dining

Castello di Pavone
Location: Pavone Canavese, Turin
Set in medieval castle battlements, dining areas occupy former archer positions. Each window frame marks historical defensive sight lines, now offering spectacular valley views.

Hidden Gems

Grotta Palazzese
Location: Polignano a Mare
Carved into limestone caves, this restaurant site has served as a noble dining venue since the 1700s. The grotto's natural acoustics create

unique sound effects from the waves below, while tables sit in positions once used for medieval summer banquets.

Monastery Views

Locanda San Fruttuoso
Location: San Fruttuoso Abbey, Ligurian Coast
Accessible only by boat or hiking trail, this restaurant in a 10th century monastery preserves dining spots once reserved for medieval pilgrims. Tables follow the path of sunlight through ancient abbey windows, creating different atmospheres throughout the day.

The essence of dining with a view in Northern Italy goes beyond mere scenery – each location tells stories through carefully preserved architectural features, historical significance, and traditional positioning of dining spaces. These restaurants don't simply offer meals with views; they provide experiences where gastronomy meets history in spectacular natural settings.

Dining Etiquette and Local Foodie Tips

Morning Rituals and Coffee Culture

The day begins with precise coffee customs espresso is taken standing at the bar before 11 AM, while cappuccino remains strictly a breakfast drink. Local bars maintain traditional "book of accounts" where regulars' coffee orders are recorded and settled monthly, a practice dating back to medieval merchant traditions. Many historic cafes still use specific cup designs that influence optimal coffee temperature and drinking patterns.

Timing and Table Customs

Lunch traditionally runs from 12:302:30 PM, while dinner rarely starts before 7:30 PM. Each region maintains specific traditions in Venice, reservations often align with church bell schedules, while mountain restaurants follow historical shepherds' dining times. The practice of "coperto" (cover charge) originates from medieval inns providing bread and table settings to travelers.

Order and Progression of Dishes

The traditional meal structure follows ancient dietary principles: antipasti (appetizers), primi (first courses, usually pasta or rice), secondi (main courses), contorni (side dishes), and dolci (desserts). Each course arrives separately requesting them together and marks you as unfamiliar with local customs. Wine selection traditionally precedes food ordering, with many restaurants maintaining seasonal pairing suggestions based on historical agricultural calendars.

Bread and Table Practices

Bread serves specific purposes beyond accompaniment; certain shapes are designed for soaking up particular sauces, while others complement specific regional dishes. The position of bread on the table often follows traditional placement patterns established in noble households. Breaking, rather than cutting, bread remains customary.

Regional Variations

In Milan, risotto alla milanese must be served on warm plates following specific temperature traditions. Venetian cicchetti (small bites) follow unwritten rules about order and combination. Mountain regions maintain altitude specific dining customs, with certain dishes traditionally served only above specific elevations.

Social Aspects

Meals represent social occasions rather than mere sustenance. Conversation between courses is expected, with specific pauses traditionally observed for digestion and discussion. Many restaurants maintain "tavoli sociali" (social tables) where solo diners can join others, following ancient hospitality customs.

Seasonal Considerations

Menu choices traditionally follow seasonal availability, ordering porcini mushrooms outside their season or seafood on Mondays (when fishing boats traditionally don't operate) marks you as an outsider. Many establishments maintain calendars showing traditional seasonal availability of ingredients.

Payment Practices

Bills are never rushed and must be specifically requested with "Il conto, per favore." Splitting bills remains uncommon in traditional establishments; historical practice involves one person paying and others settling privately later. Tipping customs vary by region, with service often included in the coperto.

Local Insights

Finding authentic experiences often means following local patterns; workers' lunch spots (traditionally open 122) often offer the best value traditional meals. Many historic restaurants maintain "secret" menus for regular customers, featuring dishes not listed but available by request.

TimeHonored Traditions

Certain dishes carry specific eating customs; risotto should be eaten from the outside in, allowing the center to maintain optimal temperature. Traditional balsamic vinegar is tasted from special spoons following ceremonies established by ancient producers' guilds.

Special Dietary Requirements

While accommodating dietary restrictions, traditional establishments appreciate advance notice. Many historic restaurants maintain special preparation areas for traditional Jewish, vegetarian, or other dietary requirements, following customs established over centuries of diverse religious and cultural influences.

Unspoken Rules

Understanding subtle customs enhances dining experiences; bread isn't traditionally eaten with pasta, olive oil isn't usually provided for bread dipping, and cheese isn't typically added to seafood pasta. These "rules" reflect historical cooking practices and regional ingredient combinations.

CHAPTER 5: THINGS TO DO AND OUTDOOR ACTIVITIES

Northern Italy's outdoor adventures weave together ancient pathways and natural wonders, from historic Alpine trails once used by Roman legions to hidden waterways that wind through preserved wilderness areas. Whether you're hiking paths between medieval villages in the Dolomites, paddling crystalline lakes where traditional wooden boats still ply their trade, or drifting silently above Renaissance gardens in a hot air balloon, each experience connects you with landscapes shaped by millennia of human interaction with nature.

The region's diverse ecosystems offer countless opportunities for discovery, where wildlife observers might spot rare Alpine ibex in high mountain meadows or track wolf populations in remote valleys using traditional methods employed by local shepherds. These wild spaces connect with carefully cultivated historic gardens where rare botanical specimens flourish in microclimates created by ancient walls, and parks where centuries old trees shade paths that once welcomed grand tour travelers.

Adventure here means engaging with both natural and cultural heritage, where proper preparation enhances appreciation of these complex landscapes. Traditional mountain weather prediction methods still prove valuable alongside modern forecasting, while local knowledge about seasonal conditions, passed down through generations of guides and farmers, helps visitors safely explore these remarkable territories where wilderness and civilization have long coexisted in delicate balance.

Hiking Trails in the Northern Italy

The Dolomites' Alta Via 1, stretching 150 kilometers from Lago di Braies to Belluno, stands as a testament to centuries of human passage through these majestic peaks. Ancient Roman paving stones still mark sections of this historic trade route, while World War I tunnels carve through mountainsides, telling stories of more recent conflicts. Traditional shepherds' huts, now serving as welcoming refugios, maintain their original architectural features were medieval travelers once sought shelter. Local guides still practice traditional weather prediction methods, reading signs from specific mountain peaks that have proven reliable for generations.

Along Liguria's coast, the Via del Sale winds inland from the Mediterranean, following paths were medieval merchants once transported precious salt to mountain communities. This 130 kilometer route preserves original distance markers carved centuries ago, while historic rest stops maintain ingenious water collection systems developed by ancient travelers. Local villages still celebrate seasonal festivals that coincide with traditional salt trading calendars, maintaining a living connection to this vital historical commerce.

The eastern shore of Lake Como harbors the intimate Sentiero del Viandante, a 45 kilometer medieval pilgrimage route connecting ancient churches and monasteries. Families have maintained these stone pathways for generations, preserving not just the trail but the knowledge of traditional maintenance techniques. The path weaves through historic grape growing terraces, passing water mills that still harness mountain streams just as they did centuries ago.

High above the Mediterranean, the Alta Via dei Monti Liguri traces the mountain ridge for 440 kilometers from Ventimiglia to La Spezia. This remarkable trail passes through unique microclimates where botanical species from the last ice age find refuge. Ancient maritime signal towers punctuate the route, silent sentinels that once relayed messages along the coast. Local communities maintain traditional trail markers using methods unchanged for centuries, ensuring modern hikers can navigate as safely as their predecessors.

The Aosta Valley's Cammino Balteo creates a 350 kilometer circuit connecting medieval castles and Roman ruins through twentyfour Alpine valleys. Here, traditional pastoral communities continue their seasonal movement of livestock along these ancient paths, while remarkable irrigation channels called rus, built centuries ago, still water high altitude meadows. This living landscape demonstrates how historical agricultural practices shape modern trail experiences.

In Trentino, the Sentiero della Pace stretches 520 kilometers along former World War I front lines, incorporating restored military paths and tunnel systems that offer unique insights into mountain warfare. Traditional Alpine guide families maintain sections of the trail using knowledge passed through generations, while mountain communities preserve stories of wartime survival techniques that influenced the development of modern trail shelters and safety practices.

Italy's largest wilderness area, Val Grande National Park, contains a network of trails threading through abandoned villages and crossing ancient stone bridges. Traditional charcoal burning sites dot the landscape, while historic smuggling routes have been repurposed as hiking paths. Local guides still employ traditional navigation methods based on natural landmarks, demonstrating how historical knowledge enhances modern trail safety.

Around Lake Garda, Monte Baldo's trails traverse what medieval botanists called the "Garden of Europe." These paths cross unique botanical zones where herbalists have gathered rare plants for centuries. Ancient shepherds' shelters maintain traditional roof designs that ingeniously collect morning dew for drinking water, while local folklore preserves stories connecting specific trail sections with seasonal celestial events.

Understanding these trails means engaging with living history, where traditional mountain wisdom continues informing modern adventure. Local communities maintain knowledge of ancient weather patterns, while specific mountain flowers serve as reliable indicators of trail conditions. Traditional rest spots, chosen centuries ago for their natural shelter, remain as relevant today as when they were first established. This rich heritage of mountain craft and knowledge transforms simple hikes into journeys through time, where every step connects present day adventurers with centuries of human experience in these remarkable landscapes.

Kayaking and Canoeing Adventures

Northern Italy is a haven for kayaking and canoeing enthusiasts, offering diverse landscapes that range from serene alpine lakes to thrilling river rapids. Whether you're gliding through the emerald waters of Lake Garda or navigating the rushing streams of the Adige River, every paddle is a chance to soak in the region's natural beauty and connect with its unique ecosystems.

Lake Garda: A Kayaker's Paradise
Lake Garda, Italy's largest lake, is a prime spot for kayaking. Its crystal clear waters are surrounded by picturesque villages like Malcesine and Limone sul Garda. Imagine paddling near steep cliffs while catching glimpses of castles perched above. Early mornings are the best time to set out, with calm waters that reflect the pastel hues of the rising sun.
occasion: Lake Garda, accessible via Verona (30 km away) or Brescia (50 km away).
Contact: Garda Adventure Kayak, Piazza Porto Vecchio 10, Malcesine.
Phone: +39 045 657 1000

The Adige River: A Wild Ride
For those seeking adventure, the Adige River offers a mix of tranquil stretches and exhilarating rapids. This river winds its way through TrentinoAlto Adige, providing a chance to paddle past vineyards, ancient Roman bridges, and charming riverside towns like Rovereto.

Unique Fact: The Adige is the secondlongest river in Italy, and its waters have been used for trade and transport since Roman times. Today, it's a hotspot for ecofriendly kayaking trips.
 Contact: Kayak Explorer Trentino, Via Dante 45, Rovereto.
Phone: +39 0464 450245

Website: www.kayaktrentino.it
Activities: Halfday whitewater adventures, ecotours, and teambuilding sessions.

Venetian Lagoon: A Paddle Through History
The Venetian Lagoon offers a onceinalifetime kayaking experience. Glide past quiet canals, vibrant fishermen's huts on Burano Island, and the striking architecture of Torcello. Unlike motorized boats, kayaks allow you to explore hidden waterways and experience Venice from a fresh perspective.

 Unique Fact: Paddling in Venice gives you access to canals that are too narrow for gondolas, uncovering a quieter side of the city that most tourists never see.
Contact: Venice Kayak, Isola di Certosa, Venice.
Phone: +39 349 151 7796
 Website: www.venicekayak.com
 Activities: Fullday lagoon tours, private excursions, and cultural paddling experiences.

 Lake Como: Romantic Serenity
Lake Como isn't just famous for its luxurious villas; its tranquil waters are perfect for kayaking. Paddle past elegant estates, charming harbors, and lush gardens. Bellagio, known as the "Pearl of Lake Como," offers a stunning backdrop for leisurely trips.

Unique Fact: Lake Como's inverted Y shape means each arm of the lake provides a distinct kayaking experience, from the quiet southern shores to the more rugged northern stretches.
Contact: Como Watersports, Via Lungo Lario 22, Bellagio.
 Phone: +39 031 950321

Website: www.comowatersports.it
Activities: Selfguided rentals, guided sunset tours, and group kayaking events.

Safety and Tips

- Always check local weather conditions before heading out, as alpine regions can be unpredictable.
- Beginners are advised to opt for guided tours to learn the basics and ensure a safe experience.
- Don't forget to bring a waterproof camera—you'll want to capture the magic of paddling under the Dolomites or through Venice's hidden canals.

With its blend of stunning scenery, rich history, and diverse kayaking opportunities, Northern Italy promises a paddling experience unlike any other.

Hot Air Balloon Rides

Hot Air Balloon Rides in Northern Italy

Imagine gently floating above picturesque vineyards, historic towns, and dramatic alpine landscapes while the sun rises or sets over Northern Italy's breathtaking scenery. A hot air balloon ride here is more than just an adventure—it's an unforgettable way to soak in the region's charm from a unique vantage point. From the rolling hills of Piedmont to the serene waters of Lake Maggiore, every moment in the air feels like stepping into a living postcard.

One of the most enchanting locations for hot air balloon rides is the Langhe region in Piedmont, known for its UNESCO-listed vineyards and rolling hills. Drifting over the lush landscapes dotted with medieval castles, such as the stunning Grinzane Cavour Castle, offers a perspective unlike any other. The autumn months are particularly spectacular, as the hills transform into a tapestry of golden and crimson hues. Operators like Balloon Piemonte (Via Roma 33, Barolo, Piedmont) provide exclusive rides that include champagne toasts and panoramic views of iconic wine-producing areas.
Contact: +39 0173 568644 | www.balloonpiemonte.it

For a mix of nature and history, Lake Maggiore offers an extraordinary backdrop. Floating above this shimmering alpine lake reveals its turquoise waters framed by the majestic Alps, lush gardens, and historic Borromean Islands. A sunrise flight unveils the beauty of this region as the morning light casts a golden glow over places like Isola Bella and Stresa. With operators like Maggiore Ballooning (Piazza Guglielmo Marconi, Stresa), riders can enjoy small group flights or private tours that capture the serenity of the lake from above.
Contact: +39 0323 30125 | www.maggioreballooning.it

The Po Valley, Italy's largest plain, offers a tranquil hot air ballooning experience perfect for those seeking peaceful views of vast fields and rivers. This area, stretching from Lombardy to Emilia-Romagna, provides stunning vistas of the River Po winding through the countryside. Flights here often pass over small villages and offer glimpses of Northern Italy's agricultural heartland. Balloon Adventures Italy (Via Emilia 45, Piacenza) is a trusted provider, offering family-friendly rides with knowledgeable guides.
Contact: +39 0523 456112 | www.balloonadventuresitaly.com

For adventure seekers, the Dolomites in Trentino-Alto Adige offer hot air balloon rides that are as thrilling as they are scenic. Rising over jagged peaks and deep valleys provides an adrenaline-filled experience with views of snow-capped mountains, alpine forests, and sparkling lakes. Winter flights are particularly magical, as the landscape turns into a snow-dusted wonderland. Dolomiti Balloons (Via Dolomiti 22, Bolzano) specializes in these high-altitude experiences, with rides that take passengers closer to the region's iconic peaks.
Contact: +39 0471 654321 | www.dolomitiballoons.it

Each hot air balloon experience in Northern Italy is carefully curated to highlight the region's diverse beauty. Safety and comfort are prioritized, with professional pilots ensuring a smooth ride. From champagne toasts to personalized tours, these adventures are as luxurious as they are breathtaking. Whether you're celebrating a special occasion or simply seeking a fresh perspective, a hot air balloon ride over Northern Italy guarantees memories that will last a lifetime.

Wildlife Spotting Excursions

Northern Italy is a paradise for nature lovers, offering a variety of landscapes that are home to some of Europe's most fascinating wildlife. From the rugged alpine terrain of the Dolomites to the tranquil wetlands of the Po Delta, wildlife spotting excursions provide an intimate glimpse into the region's rich biodiversity. These adventures are perfect for those who want to step away from bustling cities and immerse themselves in the natural world.

One of the top destinations for wildlife enthusiasts is the Gran Paradiso National Park, located in the Aosta Valley and Piedmont regions. This protected area, named after its towering peak, Gran Paradiso, is Italy's oldest national park and a haven for alpine wildlife. Visitors can spot ibex gracefully climbing rocky slopes, marmots basking in the sun, and golden eagles soaring high above. Guided excursions often take you deep into the park's valleys, such as Valsavarenche, where spotting wildlife against the dramatic mountain backdrop feels like stepping into a nature documentary.

Location: Gran Paradiso National Park, accessible via Aosta or Turin.
Contact: Gran Paradiso Park Authority, Piazza Vittorio Emanuele II 5, 11100 Aosta.
Phone: +39 0165 75301
Website: www.pngp.it

For a contrasting experience, the Po Delta Regional Park, located in the Emilia-Romagna region, offers a completely different ecosystem teeming with life. This sprawling wetland is one of Europe's most important birdwatching destinations, with over 370 species recorded. Flamingos, herons, and ospreys are just a few of the avian wonders you

133

can spot while exploring its lagoons, marshes, and canals. Boat tours and guided walking excursions provide a chance to observe wildlife up close while learning about the delicate balance of this unique habitat.

Location: Po Delta Regional Park, accessible via Ferrara or Ravenna.
Contact: Po Delta Tourism Center, Via Don Minzoni 14, Comacchio.
Phone: +39 0533 314003

Wildlife enthusiasts will find the Stelvio National Park, situated between Lombardy and Trentino-Alto Adige, to be an exceptional destination. As Italy's largest national park, it boasts a diverse range of habitats, from glacial valleys to dense forests. This is the perfect place to spot red deer, chamois, and even the elusive lynx. In winter, guided snowshoeing tours add a magical touch, offering the opportunity to track animal footprints in the snow and discover their secret hideaways.

Location: Stelvio National Park, accessible via Bormio or Bolzano.
Contact: Stelvio Park Visitor Center, Piazza Kuerc 5, Bormio.
Phone: +39 0342 911320
Website: www.stelviopark.it

For marine wildlife enthusiasts, Cinque Terre Marine Protected Area offers a glimpse into life beneath the waves. Situated along the Ligurian coast, this UNESCO World Heritage site is not only known for its stunning cliffs and villages but also for its thriving marine biodiversity. Snorkeling and diving excursions reveal colorful coral reefs, playful dolphins, and schools of fish navigating the crystal-clear waters. Expert guides ensure the experience is as educational as it is awe-inspiring.

Location: Cinque Terre Marine Area, Liguria.

Contact: Cinque Terre National Park Authority, Via Discovolo 280, Riomaggiore.

Phone: +39 0187 762600

Website: www.parconazionale5terre.it

Northern Italy's diverse wildlife experiences promise more than just sightseeing—they offer a chance to reconnect with nature in some of Europe's most stunning environments. With professional guides, eco-conscious tours, and awe-inspiring landscapes, each excursion delivers unforgettable moments that bring you closer to the region's wild heart.

Gardens and Parks to Explore

Northern Italy is home to some of the most enchanting gardens and parks in Europe, blending natural beauty with centuries of history. From lush botanical gardens to meticulously designed landscapes, these green spaces offer a serene escape and a glimpse into the artistry of Italian garden design. Whether you're a nature lover, a history buff, or simply looking for a tranquil retreat, these gardens and parks are sure to inspire.

Villa Carlotta (Lake Como)
Nestled along the shores of Lake Como, Villa Carlotta is renowned for its stunning botanical gardens. Spanning over 20 acres, this 17th-century villa boasts terraces filled with azaleas, camellias, and rhododendrons. As you stroll through the manicured paths, you'll discover sculptures, fountains, and a breathtaking view of Lake Como framed by the surrounding mountains. Spring is the best time to visit when the gardens are in full bloom, creating a vibrant explosion of colors.

Location: Via Regina 2, Tremezzo, Lake Como.
Contact: +39 0344 40405
Website: www.villacarlotta.it
Parco Giardino Sigurtà (Verona)
Located near Verona, Parco Giardino Sigurtà is a sprawling 600,000-square-meter park celebrated for its seasonal displays of tulips, roses, and water lilies. Voted one of the most beautiful parks in Europe, it offers attractions like the enchanted Maze Garden, panoramic viewpoints, and a stunning Avenue of Roses. Families will enjoy cycling through the park or taking a relaxing electric shuttle tour.

Location: Via Cavour 1, Valeggio sul Mincio, Verona.

Contact: +39 045 6371033

Website: www.sigurta.it

Isola Bella Gardens (Lake Maggiore)

Part of the Borromean Islands, Isola Bella features one of the most iconic Italianate gardens in the world. This terraced masterpiece includes intricate sculptures, exotic plants, and the famous white peacocks that roam freely. Designed in the Baroque style, the gardens are an awe-inspiring blend of symmetry and creativity, offering stunning views of Lake Maggiore.

Location: Borromean Islands, Lake Maggiore.

Contact: +39 0323 933478

Website: www.borromeoturismo.it

Giardini di Villa Taranto (Pallanza)

The Gardens of Villa Taranto in Pallanza are a botanical wonderland. Featuring over 20,000 plant species from around the globe, these gardens are a paradise for plant enthusiasts. Highlights include the Dahlia Maze, the Victoria Amazonica greenhouse, and the magnificent fountains. The garden's year-round beauty makes it a favorite spot for photographers and nature lovers.

Location: Via Vittorio Veneto 111, Verbania, Lake Maggiore.

Contact: +39 0323 556667

Website: www.villataranto.it

Parco Sempione (Milan)

Parco Sempione, a tranquil oasis in the heart of bustling Milan, provides a welcome respite from the city's vibrant streets.This 47-hectare park features tree-lined paths, picturesque ponds, and iconic landmarks such as the Arco della Pace and Sforza Castle. It's an ideal spot for a leisurely stroll, a picnic, or a paddleboat ride on the park's central lake.

Location: Piazza Sempione, Milan.
Contact: +39 02 88465788
Website: www.comune.milano.it
Botanical Garden of Padua (Padua)
A UNESCO World Heritage Site, the Botanical Garden of Padua is the oldest academic garden in the world, established in 1545. This historical gem is home to an incredible collection of medicinal plants, rare species, and modern exhibits highlighting biodiversity. Visitors can explore themed gardens, greenhouses, and the iconic circular layout that remains a testament to Renaissance design.

Location: Via Orto Botanico 15, Padua.
Contact: +39 049 8272119
Website: www.ortobotanicopd.it
Giardini Pubblici Indro Montanelli (Milan)
For a charming urban oasis, the Giardini Pubblici Indro Montanelli in Milan's Porta Venezia district offers a tranquil escape. Featuring tree-lined avenues, historic statues, and a small pond, this park is perfect for families, with playgrounds and a planetarium for kids to enjoy.

Location: Corso Venezia, Milan.
Contact: +39 02 77402242
Website: www.comune.milano.it
Parco delle Groane (Lombardy)
If you're looking for a natural retreat, Parco delle Groane in Lombardy offers sprawling woodlands and serene landscapes. Known for its biodiversity, the park is ideal for hiking, cycling, and birdwatching. Its network of trails takes you through scenic meadows and peaceful forests, perfect for those craving a connection with nature.

Location: Via della Polveriera 2, Solaro, Lombardy.

Contact: +39 02 9698141

Website: www.parcogroane.it

From historic botanical gardens to tranquil urban parks, Northern Italy offers green spaces that cater to every taste. These enchanting destinations provide not just beauty but also an opportunity to relax, explore, and discover the region's deep connection to nature and artistry.

Outdoor Adventure Tips

Exploring Northern Italy's diverse landscapes—from the towering Alps to serene lakes and lush valleys—is an unforgettable experience. Whether you're hiking, biking, kayaking, or embarking on a wildlife excursion, preparation is key to enjoying these adventures safely. Here are specific tips and precautions to ensure your outdoor adventures in Northern Italy are both thrilling and safe.

1. Plan Your Adventure Ahead

Research Locations: Understand the difficulty level of trails or activities before setting out. For example, alpine hikes in the Dolomites may require advanced skills, while walks around Lake Garda are suitable for beginners.Check Weather Conditions: Alpine weather can change rapidly, especially in regions like Trentino-Alto Adige. Always check forecasts via reliable apps like Meteo.it or local tourist offices.

Permits and Regulations: Certain areas, such as Gran Paradiso National Park, may require permits for activities like hiking or camping. Contact park authorities or visit their websites for specific guidelines.

2. Gear Up Properly

Clothing: Wear moisture-wicking layers and sturdy hiking boots for mountain trails. For water-based adventures, pack quick-dry clothing and secure footwear.

Essentials to Pack:

First aid kit

Map (physical and digital, with downloaded offline versions)

Refillable water bottle and snacks

Flashlight or headlamp for early starts or late finishes

Safety Equipment: If kayaking or biking, ensure helmets and life jackets are in good condition. Many local operators provide gear, but check in advance.

3. Be Prepared for Altitude

Acclimatization: If venturing into high-altitude areas like the Stelvio Pass or Mont Blanc, allow time to acclimate. Avoid strenuous activity immediately upon arrival.

Hydration and Nutrition: Drink plenty of water and snack regularly to maintain energy levels. Pack high-calorie snacks such as nuts, granola, or chocolate.

Recognize Symptoms of Altitude Sickness: Headaches, nausea, and fatigue are common signs. If your symptoms don't improve, go to a lower altitude right away.

4. Stay Safe in Wildlife Areas

Respect the Animals: In wildlife-rich areas like the Po Delta or Gran Paradiso, observe animals from a safe distance. Avoid feeding or disturbing them, as it disrupts their natural behavior.

Carry Binoculars: For wildlife spotting excursions, a pair of binoculars enhances your experience while keeping a respectful distance.

Insect Protection: Use eco-friendly insect repellent, especially in marshy areas like the Po Delta.

5. Navigation and Communication

Local Maps: Always carry a detailed map of the area, especially in remote regions like the Dolomites or Aosta Valley.

Phone Coverage: Be aware that mobile signals may be weak in mountainous or rural areas. Inform someone of your itinerary and expected return time.

Emergency Numbers: Save Italy's emergency number (112) and park-specific hotlines. For alpine emergencies, the Alpine Rescue Service (Corpo Nazionale Soccorso Alpino e Speleologico) can be reached at +39 118.

6. Respect the Environment

Leave No Trace: Carry out all trash, including biodegradable items, to preserve the pristine beauty of nature. Many parks, such as Stelvio and Cinque Terre, strictly enforce this principle.

Stick to Trails: Straying off marked paths can damage fragile ecosystems and put you at risk of getting lost.

Eco-friendly Practices: Use reusable water bottles and avoid single-use plastics. Many regions, including Lake Como, promote sustainable tourism practices.

7. Know Seasonal Considerations

Winter Adventures: For skiing or snowshoeing in the Alps, always check avalanche reports and consider hiring a certified guide.

Summer Precautions: Wear sunscreen, sunglasses, and a hat to protect yourself from the sun, especially in open areas like Lake Garda.

Peak Seasons: Popular spots like Lake Maggiore and Parco Sigurtà can get crowded. Visit early in the morning or during shoulder seasons for a quieter experience.

8. Use Local Guides and Tours

Certified Guides: In challenging areas like the Dolomites or Po Valley, guided tours ensure safety and provide deeper insights into the region's history and wildlife.

Reputable Operators: Choose licensed providers for activities like rock climbing, kayaking, or hot air ballooning. Check reviews and ask for certifications.

9. Emergency Preparation

Travel Insurance: Ensure your insurance covers outdoor activities like hiking or kayaking.

Local Rescue Services: Familiarize yourself with local rescue services in areas you plan to explore.

Pack an Emergency Kit: Include a whistle, thermal blanket, and multipurpose tool for unexpected situations.

With proper preparation, Northern Italy offers outdoor adventures that are as safe as they are thrilling. From the tranquil shores of its lakes to the rugged beauty of its mountains, every moment spent exploring this region will leave you with lasting memories and a deeper appreciation for nature.

CHAPTER 6: ART, CULTURE AND ENTERTAINMENT

Northern Italy is a region where culture thrives in every corner, blending history, creativity, and vibrant social life. The local arts and crafts scene is a testament to its deep traditions, with artisans producing everything from intricate lace in Venice to beautifully crafted ceramics in Lombardy. These traditions are echoed in its many museums and galleries, where masterpieces from the Renaissance and modern art movements coexist, creating spaces that inspire and captivate visitors.

Festivals and events add a lively pulse to this cultural richness, showcasing everything from centuries-old traditions to contemporary celebrations. From the dazzling Carnival of Venice to intimate local fairs in smaller towns, there's always something happening that brings people together to celebrate music, food, and community. As the day transitions to night, the region transforms into a hub of nightlife and entertainment, offering cozy wine bars, bustling piazzas, and vibrant clubs where locals and visitors mingle.

Complementing this cultural immersion are the local markets and shopping experiences that bring the region's charm to life. Wandering through markets filled with fresh produce, handmade goods, and unique souvenirs is as much about the atmosphere as it is about finding a keepsake to take home. Whether exploring historic marketplaces or stylish boutiques, every outing offers a piece of Northern Italy's soul. Together, these experiences form a colorful tapestry that showcases the region's creativity, heritage, and joie de vivre.

Local Arts and Crafts

Northern Italy's arts and crafts are a vivid expression of its cultural heritage, blending time-honored traditions with a touch of modern innovation. Each region has its own unique contributions, reflecting the diverse landscapes and histories of this enchanting part of the country. From intricate craftsmanship to bold artistic movements, the creations of Northern Italy tell stories that connect the past with the present.

One of the most iconic crafts in the region is Murano glassmaking, which has been perfected for centuries on the Venetian island of Murano. Artisans here are known for their unrivaled skill in creating colorful glassware, from delicate chandeliers to intricate beads. Visitors can witness the mesmerizing process of glassblowing at workshops and even try their hand at crafting a piece of their own. Nearby, Burano offers a different artistic treasure—its lacework. Burano lace, prized for its intricate patterns, has been a symbol of elegance since the Renaissance. Today, you can still find women weaving this delicate fabric in small studios, keeping the tradition alive.

The ceramics of Faenza, located in Emilia-Romagna, are another cornerstone of Northern Italy's craft heritage. Known as "majolica," these ceramics feature vibrant, hand-painted designs often inspired by nature and mythology. Faenza's long history of ceramic artistry is celebrated at the International Museum of Ceramics, but you'll also find plenty of workshops where you can purchase authentic pieces or learn about the techniques directly from local artisans.

In the Dolomite regions of Trentino-Alto Adige, woodcarving is a tradition deeply rooted in the alpine culture. Craftspeople create

145

everything from religious figurines to decorative household items using locally sourced timber. The craftsmanship here is renowned for its precision and beauty, often reflecting the natural environment of the mountains. Similarly, Lombardy's textile industry, centered in Como, showcases a different form of artistry. The region's luxurious silk production has made it a global leader in high-end fabrics, supplying materials to fashion houses worldwide. Visiting silk museums and ateliers in Como reveals the meticulous process behind this exquisite craft.

Northern Italy also celebrates its artistry through artisan markets, where you can find handmade goods ranging from leather goods to intricate jewelry. These markets, held in cities like Milan and Verona, provide not only a chance to shop but also an opportunity to meet the artists and hear the stories behind their creations. What makes these crafts so special is the dedication to preserving centuries-old techniques while embracing contemporary designs.

Whether it's the fiery forges of Murano, the delicate looms of Como, or the rugged carving studios of the Dolomites, the arts and crafts of Northern Italy reflect a deep connection to tradition, nature, and creativity. Every piece, from glass to lace to ceramics, carries a part of the region's soul, offering visitors a chance to bring home not just a souvenir but a piece of its history and culture.

Museums and Galleries

Museums and Galleries in Northern Italy

Northern Italy is a treasure trove for art and history enthusiasts, home to some of the world's most iconic museums and galleries. Each venue offers a journey into the past, present, or future, whether through Renaissance masterpieces, ancient artifacts, or cutting-edge contemporary art. Every museum and gallery has its own story to tell, making each visit a unique experience.

In Milan, the Pinacoteca di Brera stands as a beacon of Renaissance and Baroque art. Housed in a grand 18th-century building, it features works by Italian masters like Raphael, Caravaggio, and Titian. What makes this gallery special is its role in preserving cultural heritage during wartime; many of its masterpieces were hidden during World War II to protect them from destruction. Today, visitors can marvel at Raphael's The Marriage of the Virgin or Caravaggio's intense Supper at Emmaus while exploring the lush courtyard and historic architecture that complement the art inside.

Venice offers an entirely different experience with the Peggy Guggenheim Collection, one of the most important museums of modern art in Europe. Located in the stunning Palazzo Venier dei Leoni along the Grand Canal, this gallery showcases works from artists like Jackson Pollock, Salvador Dalí, and Pablo Picasso. What sets it apart is its intimate setting and personal history—Peggy Guggenheim herself curated the collection, living in the palazzo and championing modern art at a time when it was still emerging.

For a glimpse into Italy's ancient history, head to Turin's Egyptian Museum (Museo Egizio), considered the most important museum dedicated to ancient Egyptian culture outside of Cairo. With over 30,000 artifacts, including mummies, sarcophagi, and papyrus scrolls, it offers an unparalleled look into ancient Egypt's mysteries. The museum's crown jewel is the Tomb of Kha, an almost perfectly preserved burial site dating back to 1400 BCE, providing an extraordinary insight into daily life in ancient times.

Art lovers will find the Galleria degli Uffizi's northern counterpart in Bologna's National Art Gallery (Pinacoteca Nazionale). Housing a wealth of works by Bolognese painters, it also includes masterpieces by Giotto, Raphael, and Tintoretto. This gallery is known for its focus on regional art, offering a deep dive into the artistic movements that shaped Emilia-Romagna and beyond.

In Verona, the Museo di Castelvecchio combines history and art in a setting that feels like stepping into a medieval tale. This fortified castle-turned-museum showcases sculptures, paintings, and weapons from the Middle Ages to the Renaissance. Its unique design by architect Carlo Scarpa blends modern aesthetics with ancient architecture, creating a space that is as much an artwork as the pieces it holds.

For contemporary art enthusiasts, the MART Museum (Museum of Modern and Contemporary Art of Trento and Rovereto) in Trentino-Alto Adige is a must-visit. The museum's futuristic design reflects its innovative collection, featuring works by Italian futurists, abstract artists, and groundbreaking contemporary creators. Regularly hosting temporary exhibitions, MART ensures that each visit offers something new and exciting.

Whether it's gazing at world-famous paintings, exploring the depths of ancient civilizations, or diving into avant-garde contemporary art, Northern Italy's museums and galleries promise an enriching journey for all. Each institution is not just a collection of art but a portal into the rich cultural tapestry of Italy, where every visitor can find inspiration and connection.

Festivals and Events

Northern Italy comes alive with festivals and events that celebrate its rich history, vibrant culture, and deep-rooted traditions. From grand citywide celebrations to intimate village fairs, these occasions offer a glimpse into the heart and soul of the region. Whether you're drawn to music, food, or centuries-old customs, there's something unforgettable waiting for you in every corner of Northern Italy.

One of the most iconic festivals is the Carnival of Venice, a world-famous celebration of masks, costumes, and centuries-old pageantry. Held in the weeks leading up to Lent, this festival transforms the canals and squares of Venice into a stage for elaborate parades and private masquerade balls. Unique to Venice is the tradition of crafting intricate, handmade masks, each a piece of art reflecting themes of mystery and fantasy. The grand finale, Il Ballo del Doge, is an extravagant event that blends history with opulence, making it a must-see for visitors.

Moving to Piedmont, the Alba White Truffle Festival showcases one of the region's most prized culinary treasures. Held every autumn, this event draws food enthusiasts from around the globe. Visitors can explore bustling truffle markets, attend cooking demonstrations, and savor gourmet dishes prepared by world-class chefs. Unique to this festival is the truffle auction, where rare truffles fetch astonishing prices, reflecting their value in Italian gastronomy.

For music lovers, the Arena di Verona Opera Festival is a magical experience. Set in the ancient Roman amphitheater in Verona, this summer event brings together world-renowned opera singers and spectacular productions under the open sky. The combination of timeless music and the historical setting creates an atmosphere unlike any other, leaving audiences spellbound. A unique feature of this festival is its use of traditional candle-lit seating, which enhances the intimate and dramatic ambiance.

In Emilia-Romagna, the Ravenna Festival is a celebration of performing arts that blends classical music, dance, and theater. What makes this festival special is its focus on honoring the city's history while showcasing innovative performances. Events are held in unique venues, including ancient basilicas and historical piazzas, creating a dynamic interplay between past and present. Highlights include orchestral concerts under the stars and modern interpretations of classical works.

For a more playful experience, the Battle of the Oranges in Ivrea, Piedmont, is a thrilling and colorful event rooted in medieval history. This lively festival reenacts a historic rebellion through an epic orange-throwing battle between teams representing the people and the ruling tyrants. The atmosphere is electric during the Palio, as both participants and spectators share in the excitement. The streets are alive with a sense of community and shared enthusiasm.

Spring in Northern Italy brings the Tulip Festival at Parco Sigurtà, near Verona, where over a million tulips bloom in a dazzling array of colors. This event is not just a visual delight but also a celebration of nature's beauty, with guided tours, photography contests, and workshops. The unique layout of the park, with its rolling hills and reflective ponds, adds to the enchantment of the festival.

From epicurean delights to grand performances and quirky traditions, the festivals and events of Northern Italy are as diverse as its landscapes. Each celebration offers a chance to immerse yourself in the local culture, meet passionate people, and create memories that last a lifetime. Whether you're seeking elegance, adventure, or simply a good time, the festivals of Northern Italy will not disappoint.

Nightlife and Entertainment

Northern Italy's nightlife is as diverse and vibrant as its cultural heritage, offering a dynamic blend of experiences that cater to every mood and taste. From chic rooftop bars overlooking glittering cityscapes to lively clubs where the music pulses into the early hours, the region promises unforgettable evenings. Whether you're seeking sophistication, live music, or a more laid-back ambiance, Northern Italy's entertainment scene is ready to impress.

In Milan, the fashion and business capital of Italy, nightlife is synonymous with elegance and glamour. The city's iconic Navigli district is a hotspot for evening entertainment, with its picturesque canals lined with trendy bars and restaurants. Here, locals and visitors alike gather for aperitivo, the quintessential Italian happy hour, where drinks are served with complimentary appetizers. Unique venues like Terrazza Martini, a rooftop bar with panoramic views of the city, offer a sophisticated experience, perfect for sipping cocktails while enjoying the dazzling lights of Milan's skyline.

Venice offers a completely different flavor of nightlife, blending romance and mystery. The city's evening vibe is quieter but no less enchanting. Gondola rides by moonlight, accompanied by live serenades, provide an intimate way to enjoy the city's waterways. For those seeking a more vibrant experience, venues like Campo Santa Margherita come alive with lively bars and local music. Unique to Venice is the tradition of stopping at bacari, small wine bars, to sample regional wines and cicchetti (Venetian tapas) as part of a casual night out.

Bologna, a vibrant student city, is celebrated for its energetic nightlife and a thriving music scene.Jazz enthusiasts flock to Cantina Bentivoglio, a renowned club where live performances are paired with fine dining. For a livelier experience, head to the historic Quadrilatero district, where bustling piazzas are filled with locals sipping wine and enjoying late-night conversations. Bologna's blend of history and modernity makes it an ideal destination for those looking to explore unique venues with character.

In the Dolomites and alpine regions, the nightlife takes on a cozy, rustic charm. Après-ski parties in towns like Cortina d'Ampezzo offer a lively way to unwind after a day on the slopes. Warm mountain lodges transform into vibrant hubs with live music, hearty meals, and an array of local craft beers. The Stube rooms in Trentino-Alto Adige, traditional alpine taverns, are particularly special, offering an authentic ambiance with roaring fireplaces and warm hospitality.

Turin, with its artistic vibe, has a nightlife scene that caters to creatives and intellectuals. The city's Piazza Vittorio Veneto, one of the largest squares in Europe, is a hub of activity at night, with an eclectic mix of bars, wine cellars, and music venues. Turin also boasts unique cocktail bars like Barz8, known for its inventive drinks and atmospheric setting. Live performances, from indie bands to experimental theater, are a regular feature in this cultural city, offering a unique twist on traditional nightlife.

Northern Italy's nightlife is not just about the venues but the experiences they create. From sharing a drink with friends along the canals of Milan to dancing under the stars in the Alps or savoring wine in a Venetian bacaro, every evening tells a story. The mix of old-world charm and modern energy ensures that no two nights are the same, making this region a must-visit for anyone looking to experience Italian life after dark.

Local Markets, Shopping, and Souvenirs

Shopping in Northern Italy is an experience that combines culture, tradition, and modern sophistication. From bustling local markets brimming with handcrafted goods to high-end boutiques showcasing world-class fashion, the region offers something for every shopper. Whether you're hunting for unique souvenirs or indulging in luxury, the charm of Northern Italy's shopping scene lies in its diversity and authenticity.

The vibrant local markets are a treasure trove of discoveries. In Venice, the Rialto Market is a must-visit for its lively atmosphere and centuries-old tradition.This market, situated close to the renowned Rialto Bridge, is celebrated for its fresh seafood, vibrant produce, and handcrafted goods.A unique find here is Murano glass jewelry, delicately crafted by local artisans, and Burano lace, known for its intricate patterns and centuries of craftsmanship. These souvenirs capture the spirit of Venetian artistry, making them perfect mementos of your visit.

For a blend of history and shopping, Turin's Porta Palazzo Market, the largest open-air market in Europe, offers an eclectic mix of goods. From gourmet foods like truffles and aged cheeses to vintage clothing and home décor, the market reflects Turin's multicultural vibe. One of the market's unique features is the Balon flea market, held on weekends, where antique hunters can uncover rare finds and quirky treasures.

In Milan, the fashion capital of Italy, shopping takes on a luxurious tone. The Quadrilatero della Moda, a district of high-end boutiques, is a paradise for those seeking designer labels like Prada, Gucci, and Versace. What sets Milan apart is its commitment to craftsmanship;

many boutiques offer bespoke services, tailoring pieces to fit your style perfectly. For a more traditional experience, visit Mercato di Via Fauche, a popular street market where you can find everything from discounted designer items to handmade leather goods.

Northern Italy is also home to some of the finest culinary souvenirs. In Bologna, the Mercato di Mezzo and Quadrilatero Market are havens for food lovers, offering Parmigiano-Reggiano, balsamic vinegar from Modena, and hand-rolled tortellini. Purchasing these authentic flavors is not just about bringing home a taste of Italy—it's about supporting local producers who carry on centuries-old traditions. Additionally, the olive oil from Lake Garda and wines from Piedmont, such as Barolo or Barbaresco, make excellent gifts for friends and family.

The picturesque Christmas markets of Northern Italy, especially in Trentino-Alto Adige, add seasonal magic to shopping. In towns like Bolzano and Merano, wooden stalls offer handmade ornaments, woolen scarves, and traditional alpine treats like strudel and mulled wine. These markets not only provide unique souvenirs but also create a festive atmosphere that captures the charm of winter in the Alps.

Handmade leather goods are another highlight of the region, with Florence and Verona being well-known for their skilled artisans. From bags to belts and notebooks, these items are crafted with attention to detail, ensuring durability and timeless elegance. Como, famous for its silk industry, offers luxurious scarves and ties, woven with intricate patterns and sold in both markets and upscale boutiques.

Shopping in Northern Italy is about more than buying—it's about immersing yourself in the culture. Whether you're haggling over vintage treasures at a flea market or admiring the craftsmanship in a boutique, every purchase carries a piece of the region's story. From timeless fashion to edible delights, the souvenirs you take home will serve as cherished reminders of your journey through this enchanting part of Italy.

CHAPTER 7: 7-DAY ITINERARY IN NORTHERN ITALY

Day 1: Arrival in Milan – Exploring the Fashion Capital

Morning:
Arrive at Milan Malpensa Airport (MXP), Northern Italy's largest international gateway. After clearing customs, take a taxi or train to the city center, approximately a 50-minute journey. Check into your hotel—ideally in the Brera district for its central location and vibrant atmosphere. After a brief rest, enjoy breakfast at Pavé, a local favorite offering artisanal pastries and excellent coffee. Begin your adventure with a stroll around Piazza del Duomo, home to the magnificent Milan Cathedral (Duomo di Milano). Ascend to the rooftop terrace for panoramic views of the city and the surrounding Alps on clear days.

Afternoon:
Head to Galleria Vittorio Emanuele II, Italy's oldest shopping arcade, located adjacent to the cathedral. This architectural marvel is perfect for both high-end shopping and people-watching. Enjoy lunch at Luini Panzerotti, famous for its savory stuffed pastries. Next, visit the Pinacoteca di Brera, Milan's premier art gallery, to admire masterpieces by Caravaggio, Raphael, and Titian. Stroll through the charming Brera district, known for its cobblestone streets, boutique shops, and quaint cafes.

Evening:
Conclude your day with dinner at Ristorante Savini, located inside the Galleria. Afterward, if energy allows, explore Milan's nightlife in the Navigli district, famous for its canals and lively bars. Sip on an Aperol Spritz at Mag Cafe while enjoying the ambiance of the illuminated waterways.

Day 2: Lake Como – A Day of Elegance and Serenity

Morning:
Take a morning train from Milan to Como (approximately 40 minutes). After you arrive, take a walk through the historic center of Como. Make sure to include a visit to the Cathedral of Como, which features a blend of Gothic and Renaissance architectural styles. From there, board a ferry for a scenic ride across Lake Como, surrounded by lush hills and luxurious villas.

Afternoon:
Disembark at Bellagio, known as the "Pearl of Lake Como." Explore its narrow streets, boutique shops, and stunning lakefront. Have lunch at La Punta, a restaurant offering fresh lake fish and spectacular views of the water. After lunch, wander through the Villa Melzi Gardens, where beautifully landscaped paths wind through exotic plants and sculptures.

Evening:
Return to Como for a relaxing evening. Dine at Il Gatto Nero, a hillside restaurant with breathtaking views of the lake and city lights. Afterward, take a leisurely walk along the lakeside promenade before heading back to Milan for the night.

Day 3: Verona – Romance and History

Morning:
Depart Milan early and take a train to Verona (approximately 1.5 hours). Upon arrival, start your exploration at Piazza Bra, home to the ancient Verona Arena, a well-preserved Roman amphitheater still used for operas and concerts. Walk along Via Mazzini, a pedestrian shopping street filled with stylish boutiques and cafes.

Afternoon:
Visit Casa di Giulietta (Juliet's House), complete with the famous balcony that inspired Shakespeare's Romeo and Juliet. Have lunch nearby at Antica Bottega del Vino, one of Verona's oldest wine bars serving traditional Veronese dishes. Spend your afternoon wandering through Piazza delle Erbe, a bustling square surrounded by historic buildings and market stalls.

Evening:
Climb up to Castel San Pietro for a panoramic view of Verona as the sun sets. Dine at Ristorante Arche Scaligere, known for its refined Italian cuisine and romantic ambiance.Stroll along the tranquil Adige River before calling it a night.

Day 4: Venice – Canals and Charm

Morning:
Take a train to Venice (approximately 1 hour). Arrive at Santa Lucia Station and immerse yourself in the city's charm as you board a vaporetto (water bus) to Piazza San Marco. Begin your day by exploring

St. Mark's Basilica and the Doge's Palace, two iconic landmarks rich in history and Venetian Gothic architecture.

Afternoon:
Enjoy lunch at Osteria alle Testiere, a small seafood restaurant highly regarded by locals. Spend the afternoon exploring Venice's narrow streets and hidden corners, visiting Rialto Market for local delicacies and souvenirs. Don't miss a gondola ride to experience the city's famous canals from the water.

Evening:
Head to Campo Santa Margherita for a lively evening filled with bars and local music. Have dinner at Trattoria al Gatto Nero on the nearby island of Burano, renowned for its colorful houses and seafood dishes. Return to Venice for a peaceful evening stroll.

Day 5: Bologna – A Culinary Adventure

Morning:
Take a morning train to Bologna (approximately 1.5 hours). Begin your day at Piazza Maggiore, the city's main square, surrounded by historical landmarks like the Basilica di San Petronio. Stop by La Vecchia Scuola Bolognese to participate in a short pasta-making workshop and learn the art of crafting tortellini.

Afternoon:
Savor your handmade creations for lunch or dine at Trattoria Gianni for authentic Bolognese cuisine. Spend the afternoon exploring Quadrilatero Market, a lively hub of fresh produce, cured meats, and regional specialties. Climb the Torre degli Asinelli, one of Bologna's famous leaning towers, for panoramic views of the city.

Evening:
Bologna's nightlife is centered around its student population. Enjoy live jazz at Cantina Bentivoglio or relax with a glass of Lambrusco wine at Enoteca Italiana. The vibrant yet relaxed atmosphere of the city makes for a perfect end to your day.

Day 6: Florence – Art and Renaissance Splendor

Morning:
Depart for Florence early (train ride approximately 1 hour). Start at Piazza del Duomo to marvel at the iconic Florence Cathedral and Giotto's Campanile. Visit the Galleria dell'Accademia to see Michelangelo's David in all its glory.

Afternoon:
Have lunch at Mercato Centrale, a food lover's paradise offering regional specialties. Spend the afternoon exploring the Uffizi Gallery, home to masterpieces by Botticelli, Leonardo da Vinci, and Caravaggio. Stroll across the Ponte Vecchio, a historic bridge lined with jewelry shops, as you soak in the city's charm.

Evening:
Dine at Trattoria Mario, a beloved spot for Florentine steak. End your evening with a view of Florence from Piazzale Michelangelo, where the city lights sparkle against the backdrop of the Arno River.

Day 7: Turin – A Regal Farewell

Morning:

Take an early train to Turin (approximately 2 hours). Begin your day at Piazza Castello, visiting landmarks like the Palazzo Reale and Mole Antonelliana, home to the National Cinema Museum. Indulge in a chocolate-tasting session at Guido Gobino, a famed chocolatier.

Afternoon:

Explore Turin's elegant boulevards and arcades, stopping for lunch at Ristorante del Cambio, a historic eatery known for its refined Piedmontese cuisine. Spend your afternoon wandering through Parco del Valentino along the Po River, visiting its medieval village replica.

Evening:

Toast to your Northern Italy adventure with an aperitivo at Piazza Vittorio Veneto, followed by dinner at Tre Galline, a restaurant steeped in tradition. Reflect on your week of discovery before heading to your hotel or preparing for your departure the next day.

CHAPTER 8: PRACTICAL INFORMATION AND TIPS

Etiquette and Customs

Northern Italy is a region rich in history, culture, and tradition, and understanding its etiquette and customs can greatly enhance your experience. Italians are known for their warmth and hospitality, but they also value respect, politeness, and an appreciation for their heritage. From social interactions to dining norms, adhering to these cultural nuances will help you blend seamlessly with the locals.

Social Etiquette
Italians in the north, while friendly and welcoming, tend to have a slightly more reserved demeanor compared to their southern counterparts. Greetings are important and typically involve a handshake with eye contact and a smile when meeting someone for the first time. Among friends or close acquaintances, a kiss on both cheeks is customary—starting with the left. Always address people formally unless invited to use their first name, using titles like "Signore" (Mr.) or "Signora" (Mrs.) along with their surname.

Punctuality is more valued in the north compared to the rest of Italy. Whether for business meetings or social gatherings, arriving on time shows respect for others' schedules. If running late, it's polite to inform your host or counterpart in advance.

Dining Customs
Dining is a cherished experience in Northern Italy, and meals are seen as a time to connect and savor life. Always wait to be seated by your

host or a server, and do not begin eating until everyone is served and the host says, "Buon appetito." Cutting spaghetti with a knife or eating it with a spoon is considered improper; twirling it with a fork is the preferred method. Bread is often used to accompany meals, but avoid dipping it in olive oil unless offered, as this is not a common Italian practice.

Tipping in restaurants is not obligatory, as a service charge is often included in the bill. However, leaving a small amount—typically rounding up to the nearest euro or 5 euros for excellent service—is appreciated. When enjoying coffee, remember that cappuccinos are traditionally a breakfast drink and rarely ordered after noon. Espresso, or simply "caffè," is the preferred choice post-meal.

Dress Code and Appearance
Italians in the north take pride in their appearance, and dressing well is a sign of respect for yourself and those around you. Even casual attire is typically polished; jeans may be worn, but they are often paired with a well-fitted shirt or blazer. When visiting religious sites such as churches or cathedrals, modesty is important—cover shoulders and knees as a sign of respect.

Behavior in Public Spaces
Politeness and decorum are valued in public spaces. Speaking loudly or causing a scene is frowned upon, especially in quieter cities like Verona or Bergamo.Consider offering your seat to those in need, such as elderly passengers, expectant mothers, or individuals with disabilities, when utilizing public transportation.In queues, avoid cutting in line, as this is considered rude and will draw disapproving looks.

Cultural Traditions

Festivals, events, and family gatherings are integral to life in Northern Italy. Whether participating in the Carnival of Venice or a local wine harvest festival, showing enthusiasm and interest in traditions is always appreciated. During such events, Italians value sharing stories and connecting with others, so being open and engaging is key.

When visiting someone's home, it is customary to bring a small gift such as flowers, a bottle of wine, or sweets for the host. Avoid giving chrysanthemums, as they are associated with funerals, and always wrap gifts elegantly. Upon leaving, thank your host with "Grazie mille" and express your gratitude for their hospitality.

Language and Communication

While many Italians speak English, particularly in larger cities, making an effort to speak Italian—even a simple "Buongiorno" (Good morning) or "Grazie" (Thank you)—is highly appreciated. Italians value direct yet courteous communication, and body language often plays a significant role. Gestures are a natural part of conversation, so don't hesitate to embrace this expressive way of communicating.

Understanding and respecting these customs will not only make your interactions smoother but also deepen your connection to the culture. Embracing these practices demonstrates appreciation for Northern Italy's rich traditions and leaves a lasting positive impression on the locals you meet.

Language and Communication in Northern Italy

Language and communication are deeply embedded in the cultural fabric of Northern Italy, reflecting the region's rich history, diverse influences, and regional pride. While Italian is the official language spoken across the country, Northern Italy is characterized by its fascinating linguistic diversity, with many local dialects and languages still in use today. Understanding these nuances and adopting basic communication practices can greatly enhance your experience.

The Italian Language in Northern Italy
Standard Italian, derived from the Tuscan dialect, is spoken by the majority of the population. While Northern Italy is a cohesive region, each of its areas boasts a unique linguistic heritage.In Veneto, you'll often hear Venetian spoken among locals, a language with unique melodic tones and influences from centuries of Venetian trade and governance. In Lombardy, the Lombard dialect is common in smaller towns and villages, while Piedmontese and Ligurian languages are widely spoken in their respective regions. These regional tongues are more than just a form of communication—they are a living connection to the past, preserving cultural traditions and local heritage.

In the Trentino-Alto Adige region, the linguistic diversity is particularly striking, with German, Ladin, and Italian all holding official status. Towns like Bolzano and Merano have bilingual signs and a strong German-speaking community, a reflection of the region's history under Austrian rule. Similarly, in Friuli-Venezia Giulia, Friulian, Slovenian, and Italian coexist, making this region one of the most linguistically rich in the country.

Practical Communication Tips

While many people in urban centers like Milan, Venice, and Turin speak English, especially in the hospitality and tourism industries, it's not as commonly spoken in rural areas. Learning a few key Italian phrases can go a long way in building rapport with locals. Greetings like Buongiorno (Good morning) and Buonasera (Good evening) are polite and appreciated, while simple phrases like Per favore (Please) and Grazie (Thank you) show respect. Italians often use expressive hand gestures to complement their speech, adding a layer of emotion and nuance to communication. Observing and adopting some of these gestures can make your interactions feel more authentic.

Body Language and Expression

Italians, including those in the north, are known for their animated way of speaking. Gestures, facial expressions, and tone often convey as much meaning as the words themselves. A simple shrug, for instance, can indicate uncertainty, while the famous "finger-pinch" gesture, accompanied by a questioning look, typically means "What are you saying?" or "What's going on?" Understanding and engaging in conversations can be enhanced by being mindful of non-verbal cues.

Maintaining eye contact during interactions is important, as it shows attentiveness and sincerity. However, it's equally important to remain respectful of personal space, as northern Italians tend to be slightly more reserved than their southern counterparts. While humor and warmth are appreciated, be cautious with jokes or comments about sensitive topics like politics or regional rivalries.

Linguistic Etiquette

Addressing people formally is a sign of respect in Northern Italy, particularly in business or with individuals you don't know well. Use

169

Signore (Mr.) or Signora (Mrs.) along with the person's last name until invited to switch to a first-name basis. The formal Lei is the preferred form of address for "you" in these situations, as opposed to the informal tu, which is reserved for friends, family, or peers.

Regional Linguistic Pride

Many locals take great pride in their regional languages and accents, which reflect centuries of history and identity. For example, Venetians may use words like cio instead of the standard Italian ciao, while Friulians have unique expressions derived from their Friulian language. Acknowledging and showing interest in these differences can foster goodwill and spark engaging conversations.

Written Communication

If you need to write or message someone in Northern Italy, keep it formal, especially in professional settings. Letters and emails often begin with Egregio/a (Dear Sir/Madam) and end with Cordiali saluti (Kind regards). Italians value proper grammar and polite phrasing, so taking care with your words will be appreciated.

Learning Opportunities

If you're inspired to deepen your understanding of the language, Northern Italy offers immersive language schools and workshops. In Florence and Milan, for instance, institutions like Scuola Leonardo da Vinci provide courses in Italian language and culture, tailored for travelers. Joining these programs not only enhances your communication skills but also enriches your cultural experience.

By embracing the linguistic richness and communicative style of Northern Italy, you'll gain a deeper appreciation for the region's people and their way of life. Even a small effort to learn the language and adapt to local customs will be met with smiles and warm exchanges, leaving you with unforgettable memories of your journey.

Simple Language Phrases to Know

Learning a few Italian phrases can make your journey through Northern Italy smoother and more enjoyable. Italians appreciate when visitors make an effort to speak their language, even if it's just the basics. These phrases are grouped into categories to help you navigate different situations, from greetings to dining out. Pronunciations are included to make it easier for you to communicate confidently.

Greetings and Polite Expressions

- - Buongiorno (Bwohn-JOHR-noh): Good morning / Good day
- Use this polite greeting until the early afternoon.
- - Buonasera (Bwohn-ah-SEH-rah): Good evening
- Perfect for late afternoon or evening encounters.
- - Ciao (Chow): Hello / Goodbye
- Informal and commonly used among friends.
- - Arrivederci (Ah-ree-veh-DEHR-chee): Goodbye (formal)
- - Grazie (GRAHT-see-eh): Thank you
- - Prego (PREH-goh): You're welcome / Please (depending on context)
- Italians use this versatile word in many ways.
- - Per favore (Pehr fah-VOH-reh): Please
- Politeness is key, especially in shops or restaurants.

Basic Questions
- - Dov'è…? (Doh-VEH): Where is…?

- Use this to ask for directions, e.g., *Dov'è il bagno?* (Where is the bathroom?).
- - Quanto costa? (KWAN-toh COHS-tah): How much does it cost?
- - Che ora è? (Kay OH-rah EH): What time is it?
- - Parla inglese? (PAHR-lah een-GLAY-seh): Do you speak English?
- Useful for initiating conversations if you're unsure of their language skills.
- - Posso avere...? (POHS-soh ah-VEH-reh): Can I have...?
- Helpful for ordering or requesting items.

Dining Out

- - Un tavolo per due, per favore. (Oon TAH-voh-loh pehr DOO-eh, pehr fah-VOH-reh): A table for two, please.
- - Il menu, per favore. (Eel meh-NOO, pehr fah-VOH-reh): The menu, please.
- - Cosa mi consiglia? (COH-zah mee con-SEE-lyah): What do you recommend?
- A great way to get suggestions from locals.
- - Posso avere il conto? (POHS-soh ah-VEH-reh eel COHN-toh): Can I have the bill?
- - Senza glutine (SEHN-zah GLOO-tee-neh): Gluten-free
- -or-
- Senza lattosio (SEHN-zah LAHT-toh-see-oh): Lactose-free
- Useful for dietary restrictions.

Shopping and Markets

- - Quanto costa questo? (KWAN-toh COHS-tah KWEHS-toh): How much does this cost?
- - Posso provare? (POHS-soh proh-VAH-reh): Can I try it on?
- Essential for shopping for clothes or shoes.
- - Avete taglie più grandi? (Ah-VEH-teh TAH-lyeh pyoo GRAHN-dee): Do you have larger sizes?
- - Mi piace. (Mee PYAHT-cheh): I like it.
- A friendly way to express approval.

Travel and Directions

- - La stazione è qui vicino? (Lah stah-TSYOH-neh EH kwee vee-CHEE-noh): Is the station nearby?
- - Vorrei un biglietto per... (Vohr-RAY oon bee-LYET-toh pehr): I'd like a ticket to...
- Add your destination, e.g., *Milano Centrale*.
- - A che ora parte? (Ah kay OH-rah PAHR-teh): At what time does it leave?
- - Quanto ci vuole? (KWAN-toh chee VWOL-eh): How long does it take?

Emergency Phrases

- - Aiuto! (Ah-YOO-toh): Help!
- Use in urgent situations to call for assistance.

- - Ho bisogno di un dottore. (Oh bee-ZOH-nyoh dee oon DOHT-toh-reh): I need a doctor.
- - Dov'è l'ospedale? (Doh-VEH lohs-peh-DAH-leh): Where is the hospital?
- - Mi sono perso/a. (Mee SOH-noh PEHR-soh/PEHR-sah): I'm lost.
- Use *perso* if you're male and *persa* if female.
- - Chiami la polizia, per favore. (KYA-mee lah poh-lee-TSEE-ah, pehr fah-VOH-reh): Call the police, please.

Cultural Phrases

- - È bellissimo! (Eh bel-LEE-see-moh): It's beautiful!
- Use to compliment something, whether it's a view, art, or food.
- - Mi scusi. (Mee SKOO-zee): Excuse me.
- Perfect for getting someone's attention or apologizing.
- - Non capisco. (Non kah-PEES-koh): I don't understand.
- - Posso fare una foto? (POHS-soh FAH-reh OO-nah FOH-toh): Can I take a photo?

Fun Facts About Italian Communication

Italians often emphasize their words with hand gestures. For example, pinching your fingers together and moving them up and down expresses confusion or disbelief. Incorporating these gestures into your interactions can make you appear more natural and connected to the culture. Italians also love expressive tones, so don't shy away from putting emotion into your voice—it's all part of the charm!

175

By learning and practicing these simple phrases, you'll feel more confident navigating Northern Italy while showing locals that you value their language and culture. Even if your pronunciation isn't perfect, your effort will be warmly appreciated, and it's sure to open doors to more enriching interactions.

Health and Safety Tips for Traveling in Northern Italy

Traveling to Northern Italy is an enriching experience, but staying mindful of your health and safety ensures your trip is as smooth as it is enjoyable. With its diverse landscapes, from bustling cities to serene countryside and rugged alpine regions, Northern Italy offers unique challenges that are best navigated with preparation. Here are some practical tips to help you stay healthy and safe during your journey.

1. Stay Hydrated and Rested

Northern Italy's climate varies widely depending on the season and location. During summer, the weather in cities such as Milan and Venice can be hot and humid. It's important to stay hydrated by drinking plenty of water. While exploring alpine areas like the Dolomites, the cooler air may disguise your need for hydration, so keep a water bottle handy. Rest adequately, especially if your itinerary involves long days of sightseeing or outdoor adventures.

2. Protect Yourself from the Sun

Whether you're strolling along Lake Garda or hiking in the Alps, the sun can be strong, particularly during summer. To shield yourself from the sun, make sure to wear sunglasses, a hat with a wide brim, and sunscreen with a high SPF.Even in cooler weather, UV exposure can be significant at higher altitudes, so take precautions.

3. Use Proper Gear for Outdoor Activities

Northern Italy is a haven for outdoor enthusiasts, but safety is key. If you're hiking, ensure you wear sturdy shoes with good grip and carry a map or GPS device. For skiing in the Dolomites of Trentino-Alto Adige, always wear a helmet and ensure your equipment is in good condition.

Stick to marked trails and be mindful of weather changes, as alpine conditions can shift rapidly.

4. Know Local Emergency Numbers

Familiarize yourself with Italy's emergency services:

- 12: General emergency number
- 118: Medical emergencies and ambulance services
- 115: Fire services

Having these numbers saved on your phone can be invaluable in urgent situations. If you're in a rural or mountainous area, check for additional local rescue services, particularly for hiking or skiing.

5. Be Mindful of Food Safety

Northern Italy is known for its incredible cuisine, and trying local dishes is one of the highlights of any trip. To avoid stomach issues:

- Choose restaurants or food stalls with good reviews or a steady stream of customers.
- Ensure dairy and meat products are fresh, especially in warmer months.
- Drink bottled or filtered water in rural areas, as tap water in cities is generally safe but may taste different from what you're used to.

6. Guard Against Mosquitoes and Insects

Mosquitoes can be bothersome in wetland areas like the Po Delta or near lakes such as Lake Maggiore. Use insect repellent, particularly during the evening, and consider wearing long sleeves and pants to minimize bites. In alpine regions, ticks are a concern during hikes, so wear protective clothing and check yourself after spending time in wooded areas.

7. Stay Aware of Pickpockets

While Northern Italy is generally safe, crowded areas like train stations, markets, and tourist attractions can attract pickpockets. Keep your valuables secure:

- Use a crossbody bag with zippers.
- Avoid carrying large amounts of cash; credit and debit cards are widely accepted.
- Be cautious with your phone or camera when taking pictures in crowded areas.

In cities like Milan or Venice, you might encounter scam artists posing as helpful locals. Politely decline unsolicited assistance if something feels suspicious.

8. Stay Informed About Altitude Sickness

If your travels take you to higher altitudes in the Alps or Dolomites, be aware of the symptoms of altitude sickness, such as headaches, nausea, or shortness of breath. To prevent it:

- Ascend gradually if possible, allowing time to acclimate.
- Avoid heavy meals and alcohol during the first day at altitude.
- If you're feeling unwell, remember to stay hydrated and pace yourself.

9. Watch Your Step in Cities and Villages

Many Italian towns, like Verona and Venice, have cobblestone streets that can be slippery, especially in rainy weather. Wear comfortable shoes with good grip to avoid tripping or falling.Venice's bridges and narrow alleys often have uneven steps, so please be careful.

10. Stay Aware of Seasonal Considerations

- Winter: Roads in alpine areas can be icy, so exercise caution if driving. Carry chains or snow tires when traveling to the mountains.
- Summer: Keep an eye on weather forecasts, as sudden thunderstorms are common in the Dolomites and lakeside regions. Avoid outdoor activities during storm warnings.

11. Health Insurance and Local Pharmacies

Ensure you have travel insurance that covers medical emergencies. Pharmacies (marked with a green cross) are easily found in cities and towns, and pharmacists can provide advice for minor ailments or recommend over-the-counter remedies. In case of more serious concerns, hospitals and clinics are well-equipped in Northern Italy.

12. Respect Local Rules and Signs

Whether visiting cultural sites, national parks, or historical areas, follow posted rules and guidelines. Avoid swimming in areas marked as unsafe or crossing restricted paths in mountainous regions. This ensures both your safety and the preservation of these treasured locations.

Emergency Contacts in Northern Italy

When traveling in Northern Italy, being prepared with essential emergency contacts ensures peace of mind and safety. The region is well-equipped with an organized response system, making help accessible in any situation. The universal 112 European Emergency Number is the first number to remember, connecting you to police, fire, medical, and rescue services. This multilingual service is especially helpful for travelers, ensuring communication in English and other languages when needed.

For medical emergencies, dial 118, which connects to ambulance and healthcare services. Northern Italy's hospitals are highly advanced, particularly in cities like Milan, Venice, and Turin. Facilities such as Milan's Ospedale Niguarda Ca' Granda or Venice's Ospedale Civile SS Giovanni e Paolo provide excellent care for emergencies. Pharmacies, identifiable by their green cross sign, are readily available for minor health concerns, and after-hours needs can be met at designated Farmacia di turno (on-duty pharmacies).

In the event of theft or crime, contacting law enforcement is straightforward. The 113 State Police (Polizia di Stato) handles immediate crime-related issues, while the 112 Carabinieri, a military police force, can assist with safety concerns or more serious incidents. If your belongings or passport are stolen, filing a report (denuncia) at the nearest police station is necessary for both insurance claims and obtaining replacement documents.

Fire-related emergencies are managed by 115 Fire Services (Vigili del Fuoco), a reliable service for structural hazards or trapped individuals.

For car troubles, the Automobile Club d'Italia (ACI) offers 24/7 roadside assistance, accessible by calling 803116. Travelers venturing into the Dolomites or other mountainous regions should note the specialized Alpine Rescue Service (Corpo Nazionale Soccorso Alpino e Speleologico), reachable via 118, which provides expert assistance for mountain and cave emergencies.

Consular services are vital if you encounter legal issues or need passport replacement. Major cities like Milan host consulates for many countries, including the United States, United Kingdom, and Australia. These offices offer essential support for travelers in distress. Additionally, the Italian National Tourist Board (ENIT) helpline, reachable at +39 06 6791121, offers advice and assistance for non-emergency issues, such as lost items or travel guidance.

Being aware of these contacts and keeping them handy ensures that you can confidently navigate any challenges while exploring the beauty of Northern Italy. Whether it's medical assistance, safety concerns, or practical advice, help is always within reach.

Communication and Internet Access in Northern Italy

Staying connected in Northern Italy is relatively easy, with robust communication networks and widespread internet access ensuring convenience for travelers. Whether you're coordinating plans, navigating unfamiliar streets, or sharing your journey on social media, the region's connectivity options cater to both tourists and locals alike.

Mobile Communication

Italy's mobile network is well-developed, with major providers such as TIM, Vodafone, WindTre, and Iliad offering extensive coverage across Northern Italy. Urban centers like Milan, Venice, and Turin boast strong signals, while even rural areas and mountainous regions have reliable service, though coverage may occasionally drop in remote locations. If you're traveling from outside the EU, consider purchasing a local SIM card for affordable calls, texts, and data. SIM cards are available at mobile stores, airports, and even convenience stores, with prepaid plans that cater to short-term visitors. To use an Italian SIM card, make sure your phone is unlocked.

International travelers can also take advantage of roaming agreements if their home carrier provides coverage in Italy, though costs can vary. For EU residents, roaming charges within Italy are generally the same as in their home country, thanks to EU regulations.

Internet Access

Internet access in Northern Italy is widespread, with most hotels, cafes, and restaurants offering free Wi-Fi. In major cities, Wi-Fi hotspots are common in public areas like train stations, libraries, and piazzas. For example, Milan and Venice provide free public Wi-Fi networks that are

183

easy to access with a quick registration. Some rural areas and smaller villages may have limited Wi-Fi availability, so planning ahead is advisable if you need constant connectivity.

For travelers requiring reliable and fast internet on the go, portable Wi-Fi devices are a great option. These pocket-sized routers, available for rent at airports or online, allow multiple devices to connect and provide uninterrupted internet access, even in remote locations.

Tips for Staying Connected
When accessing public Wi-Fi, use caution to protect your data. Avoid connecting to unsecured networks and refrain from entering sensitive information, such as credit card details, unless you're on a trusted connection. Using a VPN (Virtual Private Network) adds an extra layer of security, particularly if you rely on public hotspots.

For making calls, apps like WhatsApp, Skype, or Viber are widely used in Italy for free voice and video calls over Wi-Fi. Many locals prefer WhatsApp for communication, so downloading the app before your trip can help you stay in touch with new acquaintances or local guides.

Navigating with Technology
Smartphones are indispensable for navigating Northern Italy's cities and countryside. Apps like Google Maps, Citymapper (for public transportation), and Trenitalia (for train schedules) are invaluable tools. Download maps offline for areas where internet access might be limited, such as in the Dolomites or smaller villages. Translation apps like Google Translate, with downloadable Italian language packs, can assist with communication when language barriers arise.

Postal Services

For those who prefer traditional communication, Italy's postal service, Poste Italiane, is reliable for sending postcards or letters. Post offices are present in most towns and cities and usually operate during standard business hours, though rural branches may have limited hours. Stamps can also be purchased at tabaccherias (tobacconists), which are often marked with a "T" sign.

Emergency and Information Lines

In case of emergencies, having reliable communication is crucial. Dial 112 for all-purpose emergency services. Additionally, tourist information centers in major cities provide free Wi-Fi and resources for staying connected while traveling.

With its modern communication infrastructure and accessible internet services, Northern Italy ensures that you're never far from a signal or a connection. Whether you're sharing your adventures online, coordinating plans, or seeking assistance, staying connected has never been easier.

Useful Apps, Websites, and Maps for Traveling in Northern Italy

Traveling in Northern Italy is easier than ever, thanks to a variety of apps, websites, and maps designed to enhance your experience. From planning your itinerary to navigating public transportation, these tools help ensure a smooth and enjoyable journey. Here's a selection of resources to keep at your fingertips as you explore the region's vibrant cities, serene lakes, and majestic mountains.

Transportation and Navigation
Navigating Northern Italy's efficient transportation system is seamless with the right apps. For train travel, Trenitalia is an indispensable tool. The app provides schedules, ticket booking, and updates for Italy's national rail network, covering popular routes like Milan to Venice or Florence to Turin. Another excellent option is Italo Treno, ideal for high-speed train travel between major cities. Both are user-friendly and allow online ticket purchases. Visit www.trenitalia.com and www.italotreno.it for more information.

For city navigation, Google Maps is a reliable choice, offering detailed routes for walking, driving, and public transportation. In cities like Milan, Venice, and Bologna, Citymapper is particularly useful for its real-time updates on buses, trams, and metro systems. Be sure to download maps offline for areas with limited internet access, such as rural villages or alpine trails.

If you're driving, the Waze app helps with real-time traffic updates and alternate routes, while ViaMichelin (www.viamichelin.com) is great for route planning and includes information on toll costs and fuel prices.

Accommodation and Dining

Finding the perfect place to stay or dine is easy with apps like Booking.com and Airbnb. Both provide a wide range of accommodation options, from luxury hotels in Venice to cozy chalets in the Dolomites. For unique and local experiences, consider Agriturismo.it (www.agriturismo.it), which specializes in farm stays and countryside retreats, offering an authentic taste of rural Italian life.

When it comes to dining, The Fork (www.thefork.com) is an excellent resource for discovering top-rated restaurants and securing reservations. The app often includes discounts and user reviews, making it a go-to for food enthusiasts. For a more local touch, TripAdvisor (www.tripadvisor.com) helps you find authentic eateries, cafes, and bars across Northern Italy, complete with traveler reviews and insider tips.

Tours and Attractions

If you're planning to explore Northern Italy's iconic landmarks and cultural sites, apps like GetYourGuide (www.getyourguide.com) and Viator (www.viator.com) offer curated tours, skip-the-line tickets, and unique experiences. From guided gondola rides in Venice to wine tours in Piedmont, these platforms simplify your sightseeing plans.

For hiking or outdoor adventures, Komoot (www.komoot.com) and AllTrails (www.alltrails.com) provide detailed maps and routes for exploring Northern Italy's mountains, lakes, and national parks. Both apps include user-generated reviews and tips, ensuring you're well-prepared for the trails.

Language and Translation

Overcoming language barriers is simple with tools like Google Translate (www.translate.google.com), which offers real-time translations and offline language packs. Another option is Duolingo (www.duolingo.com), a fun and interactive app for learning basic Italian phrases before or during your trip. Both apps are invaluable for communicating with locals and enhancing your cultural experience.

Weather and Emergency Alerts
Stay informed about weather conditions with Meteo.it (www.meteo.it), a reliable app and website for regional forecasts, including detailed updates for specific areas like the Dolomites or Lake Garda. For mountain regions, Avalanche.org (www.avalanche.org) provides essential alerts and safety information, particularly useful for winter travelers.

Local Experiences and Shopping
For discovering local events, markets, and cultural activities, Eventbrite (www.eventbrite.com) and Couchsurfing (www.couchsurfing.com) are excellent options. These platforms connect you with unique experiences and local communities. If you're looking for handmade souvenirs or Italian specialties, Etsy (www.etsy.com) and Eataly (www.eataly.com) showcase a variety of artisan goods and gourmet products from Northern Italy.

Custom Maps and Guides
For a personalized touch, create custom maps using Google My Maps (www.google.com/mymaps). This tool allows you to pin locations, add notes, and organize your itinerary visually. Another great option is Maps.me (www.maps.me), which offers offline maps and navigation tailored for travelers exploring less-connected areas.

With these apps, websites, and maps, traveling in Northern Italy becomes a breeze. Whether you're planning every detail or improvising as you go, these tools offer the information and flexibility you need to make the most of your adventure. Keep them handy and enjoy a worry-free journey through one of Europe's most captivating regions.

CONCLUSION

As you wrap up this guide to Northern Italy, I hope you feel a sense of excitement and curiosity about everything this incredible region has to offer. From the artistic masterpieces of Milan and Venice to the serene beauty of Lake Como and the dramatic peaks of the Dolomites, Northern Italy is a place where every corner tells a story. Its rich history, vibrant culture, and breathtaking landscapes create an experience that's as diverse as it is unforgettable.

Northern Italy is more than just a destination—it's a blend of tradition and modernity, where centuries-old customs thrive alongside cutting-edge fashion, design, and innovation. Whether you're exploring bustling markets, savoring a freshly made plate of risotto, or marveling at the craftsmanship behind a Murano glass creation, there's a magic here that feels personal. It's in the warmth of a shopkeeper's smile, the quiet beauty of a countryside vineyard, and the lingering notes of an aria in Verona's ancient arena.

This guide has walked you through some of the region's most treasured offerings—its iconic landmarks, local traditions, culinary delights, and practical tips to help you navigate your journey. But the true charm of Northern Italy lies in the unexpected. It's in the narrow alleys you stumble upon, the locals you meet, and the unique memories you create. Every experience here has the potential to surprise and inspire, whether you're admiring Renaissance art, enjoying an aperitivo by a quiet canal, or breathing in the crisp air of an alpine trail.

Now, it's time to personalize this guide and embark on your own Northern Italian adventure. The cities and countryside are ready to welcome you with open arms and reveal their hidden gems. So pack your bags, practice a few Italian phrases, and prepare for an unforgettable journey. Whether you're a first-time visitor or a seasoned traveler, there's always something new to discover. The beauty, culture, and spirit of Northern Italy await you. Start planning your trip today—I promise it will be an experience that stays with you forever.

Printed in Dunstable, United Kingdom

66958345R00111